Freedom's Where I Wanna Be

By
Kevin Wiggins
aka
Mysfit The Lostboy

Freedom's Where I Wanna Be
Copyright © 2012 by Kevin "Mysfit" Wiggins
Mysfit87@yahoo.com

Cover design by Chyna Blue for Edifyin' Graphix

Published by Hip Hope Publishing
hiphopepublishing@gmail.com

ISBN- 978-0-9834739-3-0

Without limiting the rights under the copyright reserved above, no part of this publication may be reproduced, stored in or introduced into retrieval system, or transmitted, in any form, or by any means, without the prior written permission of the copyright owner and publisher of this book.

I dedicate
each and every piece to any human being who's ever existed in these stories.
Those who can find themselves in this poetic allegory and allow me to steal their hearts for a moment so that they can be free, this is for you.
This is your emancipation
sealed in love, blood, sweat, tears, and fears of a mysfit.
This is penetration beyond skin that goes deeper than bones to capture the souls of the broken,
a token of my appreciation.
Just in case, if no one ever told you, you are appreciated.
This is passionate rhyme and cadence structured upon pages for those who had faith in it,
for those who had faith in me.
But more importantly this is a testament to growth and confidence in a gift that brings death to insecurity.
This is for the queen who birthed the lostboy, who wrote these stories.
I hope that she'll be proud of me.
This is a dedication to my aunt, Angela Langley, who has always believed in me.
This is for my friends and family.
My special co-workers from M&T.

Elbi,
I dedicate this to you for nurturing the seeds that built my poetry and presence, powerful and strong as a tall tree.
Praises to the almighty
and last but not least
I'd like to dedicate this to hate.
To that displaced individual within, who traveled this journey of self discovery and learning to love himself this is for you.
Mysfit The Lostboy.... We've made it...

Who Is The Mysfit?

Mysfit The Lostboy was born Kevin Wiggins Jr. He was raised in a household that was close in space but emotionally distant. Through years and tales untold he would eventually come to discover why. Often finding himself hiding in bedroom closets to drown out the hell that resided in his residence, Kevin discovered the beauty in imagination and the comfort in the gift of writing and song.

With childhood dreams of becoming a singer, he exposed his vocal abilities early and began singing in church choirs, at neighborhood block parties, family functions and elementary school programs. Determined to make his dreams come true, as a teenager, he aligned himself with management responsible for many of Baltimore's musical successes. This lead to Kevin earning a place as a fixture in many local groups, which he was responsible for writing songs and allotted much time spent alone with his pen, his pad and his thoughts. Many, of which, he didn't understand. The songwriting soon evolved into poetic testaments of his own existence and soon after the passion for music birthed a new love for poetry.

The safe haven that the closet once represented to him as a child was now found in a pen's ink and the timing was perfect for a teenager, who always felt awkward and weird. Kevin never knew exactly where his place was in the world. He was uncertain of where he'd fit in but he was sure that he wanted his words to be heard, so he embraced those qualities about himself that made him feel out of place and took to the stage as Mysfit The Lostboy.
Known to be a story teller, in 2008 Mysfit The Lostboy was published in an Urban Anthology titled "Hood 2 Hood" at the age of 21. He continued to write and began performing his work on stages of many of Baltimore's Poetry venues. His impressive word play, delivery, depth of passion and power encompassed in his work brought about many request's for him to perform at many different events throughout the city, such as, benefits for the homeless, fashion shows, art gala's and peace rallies.

In 2010, Mysfit The Lostboy discovered blog talk radio and started performing his work on line and on air for lovers of the craft throughout the world. It was there, where he met many of his poetic counter parts. In 2011 at the age of 24, Mysfit The Lostboy had the honor to perform an original piece at the legendary poet and musician Gil Scott Heron's tribute celebration at the Reginald F. Lewis museum in Baltimore MD. It was around that time when he truly realized the affect that his poetry possessed. With many requests for a poetry book, he began considering the idea.

In 2012, he performed at Morgan State University for a benefit of individuals who were victims of human trafficking. Finally in April of 2012, Mysfit The Lostboy accepted the 30/30 challenge . A challenge that suggests for each of the 30 days of the month, a new poem will be written. Unaware that a book deal was up for grabs, at the end of the challenge, a friend suggested he enter the competition for the book deal. Kevin wanted the world to feel his heart. The results were "Freedoms Where I Wanna Be" A Mysft's Poetry.

Murder/Genocide

IMurder
IGenocide
IMurder
IGenocide
IMurder
IGenocide
I put aside life
I decide strife
I delight in gripe
I darken light
I Forge fatalities
Signatures upon death threats, endorsed murderous checks, which
paid the wages of evil's salary
Pay me in genocide
I am evil
Pay me with casualties of genocide
I'll receive them
Pay me with the loss of life
Pay me with generations lost in the dark of night
I am genocide and I am not decided or partial upon any particular
group of people
I practice tolerance, I'm open to all individuals, my acceptance is
equally lethal
Its, tragic if you trust me
Trust me
I'm lusting
I lust for skin
I lust for bone
I lust for bodies

I lust for souls
I lust for the tears of those broken by bloodshed
I am bloodshed
I am bodies
I intercept heartbeats
I am robbery
I am vacant
No heart of my own
I am the calendar's four seasons
But all of them are cold
See IMurder
IGenocide
IMurder
IGenocide
IMurder
I am Genocide
I've sold America my soul so pay me with warm blooded beings
I am genocide
Pay with cashed in insurance policies, funeral homes and deacons
I am Nightmare
I rid sleeping
I am reality
Purge daydreaming
I am creeping
In your home
I am Murder One
Or in droves
I am integrated, No barred holds
I am segregation, with the removal of bodies from souls
Because I am Murder
No specific group or characteristic I know
Because you all taste like Genocide

I seek to swallow humanity, as a Whole
See IMurder
IGenocide
IMurder
IGenocide
IMurder
IGenocide
Because I
Am
Murder

I Want A Poet

I want a passionate Poet
Not a popularity pageant imposter of the gifted, supermodel type poser
But a modern day griot who shares their gifts because the growth of humanity is their focus
No more of that 2nd grade hocus pocus
I want my poet to be the dopest
Like supercalifragilisticexpialidocious
One who doesn't have to constantly give themselves praise and brag about big names because their purpose is not to acquire celebrity or fame, but to let blessing rain down through their spit
I want my poet to be so sick, that once they are done kissing similes, they leave me with mononucleosis
I want their words to stick to me like gravity and messages on "post its"
I'm hoping to find potency in their words, as they strong arm metaphors nouns and verbs, rolling them up on papers like herbs sealed with the delivery of your spit so I can get high on it
No illegal narcotics, no airplanes and no pilots and yet I still find cloud nine on it
I want to dine on your lines and let your knowledge become my nourishment
Eat of the fruit of your intelligence and let your wisdom starve my ignorance
I want my poet to bleed ink through their pigment
Burn every dictionary in the world and become a breathing definition of passion and poetry
Written unselfishly, and spoken relentlessly.

I want a poet, who stops my heart, causing me to flat line when they speak
Spit orgasms, fertilize seeds and birth revival through their ink
One who drinks of the fluids of amniocenteses
Giving me a sample of life when they write because living is their thesis
See I need this poet to be aroused and wet with wisdom
Go so hard, that they become erect when spitting them; lines made to inspire, so good, that I desire to kiss the lyrics as they dismiss them
I need my poet's pen to represent their hearts sincerity
In their words, I'll seek and find therapy
A degree is no necessity, as long as, I can find healing in their written composition; prescription of poetry
And it doesn't matter if you're male or female, beauty or beast
I just want a poet, who bleeds genuine ink

Pain On Paper

Advances on the surface so vivid that the blind man could see
But she couldn't see his faults because she couldn't see past his anatomy
And it saddens me that she chose a fuck over her flesh
Her daughter forced to sleep with one eye open because this man wants to have sex
And sex is ok as long as it's consented by two individuals
What he wanted was wrong
The evidence was clear
No way could this be inadmissible
See, he was fucked up mentally
So he wanted to fuck her mentally
And he wanted to fuck her physically but she wouldn't let him
Frustrated because her legs, she wouldn't spread em', so he stabbed her
Five staples in her head because he couldn't have her
And what's sad is, her mother will still have him
Six years later and she's forced to revert back to the memory of where the pain begins and it almost breaks her
Losing her mother to the man who tried to molest and rape her
Causing her mother to denounce her role, as the one who was to protect and save her
Who signed these papers and approved this deal
If it wasn't for GOD's grace your daughter could have been killed
To not be sensitive to her circumstance, you got to have a heart of steel
And unlike you, she's not stainless like pistols or revolvers
It's like a round has been let off in her heart because her mom disregards her
As if she's swept the pain under the rug

Is she supposed to forget that, for a man you've sacrificed your flesh and blood?
Yeah, what he did was wrong, but it's just as bad not having a mother's love
Because love truly wouldn't allow this
Jeopardizing your child's safety for the presence of a coward
And by her hurting, it's so easy for hate to be devoured and become the fuel for her rage
And lately, she doesn't seem to have a whole lot to say but beware, because silence can be deadly
And I wouldn't blame her if she castrated his balls with machetes
Because he broke up her family
And that broke up her heart
Her pains on this paper, because from her lips these words wont depart
So I guess for you her silence is golden
But imagine the bottled up pain that her souls been with-holding
Memories lodged in her brain like time has been frozen
And the pain is still growing
Because her brother's growing up in that same house
With that same man and same mother
Fighting a losing battle because mother won't sacrifice lover
Therefore the child suffers and the mental stability pays the cost
To be with this man she'll risk everything
Not caring that the bond with her children be lost
Now tell me
Is that product really worth the cost?

The Fate of a Fiend

*Not even
21 years old and he's lost all of his goals to the toxins of the white shit
he snorts through his nose
He's a fiend
Chasing the white like hustlers chase green
Chasing a hit in the way that the Jacksons chased a dream
But what happened to his dreams, self-worth, morals, and pride?
Now he offers the dope boy a blow job, so he can get a dime bag for
five
He feels it keeps him alive
Without his lethal taste of ecstasy, he doesn't know how to survive
But inside, when he comes down off of his high, he feels less than a
penny when they were worth something back in the day
He prays that one day it'll be ok and he can find his way back to
sobriety
That he can kick his addiction in its entirety, but it's entirely too hard
for him to stay clean
So he runs back to the corner that's claiming his life and his esteem
He wants to go home but his mother doesn't trust the mindset of a
fiend
Besides
He never felt any love from her anyway
As a kid, she beat him like a master who's caught a slave that ran
away
So he stays away because she can't even sympathize
And he finds himself on his cousins' doorstep in the dead of winter,
with holes in his clothes and tears in his eyes
He says "I'm hungry"
"And I have no place to go"*

And his cousin does his best to feed him and shelter him from the cold
And although he has no place of his own, he offered him blankets,
clean clothes and the back seat of the car that he owns
He appreciates the generosity
But he still feels sad, misunderstood, lost and alone
Left all alone to fall deeper into his depression and addiction
Trying to find solace through his affliction
He fulfills the prediction
Another black man fated as an overdose victim...

Intangible

As you fly the friendly skies, I'm left here wishing that hugs and kisses could embrace and taste, long after minutes and days of separation
As time goes by, I still want your kiss's taste to state claim to my lips
I want to consistently take sips of your skin's scent and inhale your pheromones so like oxygen I continue to breathe you while you're gone
See I've taken mental pictures of your face but memories are intangible, I need to feel you
Thoughts that I imagine are simply fantasies of my realities, imitation of life, but I need the real you
I need to feel your skin
Pressed close up against mine
As we look into each other's eyes and become mesmerized
Getting lost in time
As fingertips roam lips
And foreign languages speak, and tongues grip a French kiss, and hand slips grazes neck napes and thighs
And I become paralyzed just to feel you breathe on me
Breaking out into hives like your some type of bad reaction of an allergy
I would work 365 days a year just to be compensated, you as my vacation, tips, 401 K, gross wages, benefits and salary
And although you're currently traveling, I would give anything just to interlock my fingers into yours and watch my joy play out in the beautiful brown eyed double screens of your pupils
But my wishes are futile because you are not here
Although your presence is ever present in my heart, I just want to feel you near
I want to hold you tight and engulf myself in my favorite genre of music, your heartbeat, singing beautifully in my ear

As I steer through the streets in this late spring heat, I see lovers and their public expressions of affection and I miss you
Longing for the day that I can reconnect with the soul that I've fallen for and bestow my passion upon your physical
Yearning to be displaced in you
Captivated by your smile, tranquilized by your kiss
Realizing that when I get lost in you, I rediscover myself in my bliss
I miss you...

Bullets

Baltimore city
Has turned into some catastrophic metropolis
Suffered a metamorphosis that adopted this idea that made men out of metal, instead of metal out of men
Placed heat and steel between metacarpals, which gave false strength and courage to cowards
Like the almighty when he arose on the third day, they felt resurrected with hands full of power
Which, only had the power to birth a genocide
Generate a homicide
And perpetuate our suicides through the vision of blinded eyes because we have yet to realize that by killing each other, we are simply killing ourselves
The black man is the new endangered species, hunted prey that's also the predator, as well
This is cannibalism of one's self
Swallowed whole by murder weapons, extracted heat, bullet wounds and bullet shells
Leaving remnants of male life forms in caskets or in urns upon shelves
The welfare of the black man is no longer well
And the women are becoming sickened by this contagion
Burying their men seemingly, as often as, they take breaths is a suffocating occasion
Boys left with no father figure turn to the concrete of these corners and the streets are left to raise them
Funeral homes are so profitable because in every life taken we're losing generations
The measure of a man's life can't be sufficed so for murder there is no reparations

But only bullets and the weapons that were used to take them
Bullets and the tombstones that's left to commemorate them
But why spit bullets designed to eliminate when you can educate them
That's why I spit bullets, the fire that can save a city!
So that our city can save a nation

When Sleeping is no Longer Peaceful (Death to Rest)

When sleeping is no longer peaceful
I wake up, kicking and screaming
Fighting nonexistent beings that are ever present in the form of problems that are living within my reality
Constantly I'm battling
My subconscious can't dodge these things, so they follow me into slumber
Comfort is a blunder, like a mistake that never happens
Perfected passion on discontentment and a lack of comfortablity
So I willingly and consistently fight that of which my eyes can't see
Fighting against my mentality because I don't want these poisons to swallow me
See the ideology often times suggest that sleeping brings serenity
But my sleeping and my peace has yet to find an affinity
I'm gripping sheets and pulling my hair
Not resting although I'm sleeping
I'm still fighting thin air
There's demons here... that I just can't see
They're grabbing and touching ...they want to marry me
They want us to be united but I'm opposed to a union that contradictory of unity
Juxtapose to their position because they're anti-peace, and I'm on a quest for tranquility
A triathlon is my sleep because a nap turns into a test of my endurance and agility
Exercising my abilities to escape these things that haunt me
Despite my prayers, I've been fighting eternally throughout my life... and in my sleep
I've become acquainted with the powers of a restless Slumber

And I wonder
Will I have to die... to rest in peace?

Shadowboxer

Boxing with shadows
But present are apparent scars left by invisible lasso's
Extended elbows to connect blows with visible nothings

But these demons aren't bluffing we're just looking with ignorant eyes
Disguises reprised in mirrors, as we stare at menacing reflections

"The calls are coming from the inside of the house our souls beckon to be
Begging to be free but yet we're fighting for our traps
Lapse into stories of our ancestry
Stories of slavery and find gashes in skin

But no more are we just fighting the white man, we're boxing with shadows and demons within
Trojan like warriors and hard dick in armor

Never under estimate the opposition in a war "This is Sparta"
No longer can we barter with our captors
They'll swallow you whole like diaphragms retaining a regurgitated laughter

Then plaster our souls upon milk cartons...LOST... as to ferment our fuckery

We make sacrifices for vices; these living organisms are all devices of our enemy... and sometimes its ourselves

Willingly we submit, and dip our person into pure poison

Hoisted up and held high on the highest of the lowest thrones

We claim to be happy but this doesn't even feel like home
This doesn't even feel like self, only the darkness of shadows

We de-throne ourselves when we perjure our power
Leaving ourselves open and available to the malice of that of which would like us devoured
Scouring particles of dirt and dust just to rediscover us
Searching for GOD and searching the latter
Searching for Adam

Searching for the atoms and the power of a man, made human;
boxing unseen opponents
Trying to regain ownership to the rights of who we are
Shadowboxing for the identity our own shadow, unrecognizable beyond our scars

Corporate King

Sensible
Civilized corporate King

It's always been my dream to be a part of the team

Wanted to be the black man that exceeds the mailroom and becomes an
Executive of that fortune 500 company, so I studied hard

Came from nothing but pennies with holes in them and hand me down garb
But momma always told me that I could make it if I applied myself and put a little faith in GOD
And faith and determination bred a prestigious college graduate
Well mannered, disciplined, suave, and articulate

Far from perfect but not once did I ever receive a failing grade
Life was a struggle growing up so I settled for nothing less than great
See I had a plan
I wanted to be a grade A man, so I accepted nothing less than A's
Maintained nothing less than a 4.0 GPA
Graduated Summa Cum Laude

So why, am I stuck… in the mailroom?
This doesn't coincide with my resume'

I told my mom that she'd no longer have to pay rent because I would buy her a house but I can't do that on this 12 dollar an hour pay

Been prompt everyday

Conducted myself properly and yet they still turn me away
You know what? fuck HR, I'm going to the executives to see what they have to say
Freshly Pressed, double breasted suit, tie and cuff links the next day

Elevator straight to the top floor
Ding!
Slides open mechanical doors, as my eyes explore all of the answers to why... I don't qualify

Black man only good enough to grease the machine but never will he operate
Was always told to go to college if he wants to achieve something great
Like outstanding student loans with interest that grow just to perpetuate the funding of our own slavery

With all that I've achieved and my name on college degrees, it was corporate America not college, to show me that there's no room at the top for me

Because no matter how educated I am, I'm still a nigger
I step into the office of this executive and see why no one has decided to hire me

Extending my arm to shake his hand and he doesn't even acknowledge me
Just nods his head and asks can he help me

He doesn't even offer me a seat
I place my resume on his desk and suggest that he check my application history, to see that I've applied for over 20 open positions within the company

Without even acknowledging my credentials he says "I see, but you don't qualify"
I simply ask why?
He says "because the mailroom is where you seem to thrive"
"It's more suited for your kind"
But I have skills... I... I qualify

I was supposed to buy my mother a house
He stopped me mid sentence and said
"Now that we're done here, you can show yourself out"
In that moment I blacked out and recognized my murder weapon in the form of a paper weight on his desk and I lashed out
Heavy blows to his skull until his blood and brains oozed out
America sold me false dreams and a college degree, but murder is the case that they gave me
A life sentence replaced the corporate dreams of a King

Now he'll never afford his Queen a house

Comfortable Hell

Comfortably sleeping in your hell
Afraid to move because you're scared to find a higher place to dwell
So therefore you don't propel and you remain content in your condition
It's like your mind is paralyzed unable to move from one position
You're somehow appeased in this affliction
Cowardly in reality, because you choose not to accept your life's mission
But listen
Nothing from nothing, leaves nothing, and nothing to nothing doesn't give anything
GOD's got a plan for your life, you've just got to open up the door and accept the delivery
And intend to be something bigger than what the world has intended for you
Remember that no man, has not a heaven or hell to throw you into
So if ever you fail then who's to judge
But if you don't attempt to try, you won't have the chance to succeed or falter because you haven't attempted to budge
You've been comfortably sleeping in your hell
Comfortable with its taste
Comfortable with its smell
Therefore you accept minimalism and the mediocrity in which you excel
Comfortable with nothingness as life passes you by
Content burning in the pits although you'd really like to fly
But instead of attempting to take to the sky
You let your dreams succumb to the fire, and misery becomes your happiness's demise

Mental Mass Destruction

Sharpshooters of the mind are starting to take toll
Crippling my future and working on my soul
Paralyzed stiff
Rock solid are the mental barriers I've built
You've sabotaged me
Now I hope that one day, they will weather away and wilt
But right now, I need someone to rescue me
Save me from my mind, where insecurities explode like landmines
Negativity lurks in each hallway, behind each door
Mind battling heart, leaving me weak and sore from this internal war in my mind
In my mind
In my mind
In my mind there's a battleground
By me I've been gagged and bound
I'm holding myself hostage and have yet to be released
Strangled by my own strongholds and taunted by my minds enraging beast
This is crazy
I'm beating on me like a stranger in the streets
Abusing myself, hoping that either my heart or my mind will retreat
Or give way to my soul and allow me to just be
And if there's any hope for my future, I'd like to exist without any bars on my heart
Clean and clear out the rubble from the mental mass destruction and allow true love to start
See, I'm not a prisoner of war...
But a prisoner of my past
No elaborate war stories

But mental uncertainty, proves to last
And the mental scarring is apparent whenever love is introduced
But since it's previously failed me, it's quickly rejected, so heartache
can live barren to me
Unable to reproduce

Fueled By the Government

She can only sell her pussy if Uncle Sam's getting a profit
If not she's making illegal, dirty money and she's labeled as a prostitute
But bring a camera in the room, record the act, to distribute to mass and its labeled "legal business"
The same business that would otherwise get her arrested and labeled worthless, is now ok as long as it serves the purpose of the government
As long as they can be taxed, then it's ok for her to turn tricks because it's not all for her own sole benefit
She can suck dick to pay her rent, as long as her spit it considered legitimate
And her pussy can't be tax exempt because, according to the government pussy's not a non-profit
A bit of a contradiction because the same America who's telling little girls not to sell their bodies is telling them to place them into the porn industry so that the whole world can buy it
And "no you won't be seen as harlot"
"You'll become a celebrity, porn star, starlet"
One who's dying in infamy...as her ass is waxed, and self worth is taxed
All the while being memorialized on VHS and DVD
On magazines and TV screens
Doing all the things that she did in the streets, that's caused her to be viewed as a criminal and renamed as dirty
Is now ok as long as it's done publicly, and the government can share in her earnings
Being pimped by the most suspicious pimp with no convictions, America's her Daddy

*One who takes her off of the corners and places her into productions,
so that he can still get his portion
No benefits, but she's subject to career sex, pregnancy tests, std's and abortion
Its legalized extortion
As the system forces her mouth wide open and fucks her face right before her own eyes and the eyes of the public
But the only difference is this time it's legalized because now when she spreads her thighs, she's being fucked by the government*

The Resume' of Violence

I've taken lives
Killed people and molested your daughters
Kidnapped your fathers
Tossed babies into waters
I've carried out the act of your sons being slaughtered
Then walked into the funeral to have you emotionally bothered
I'm the reason that police leave innocent citizens slain in the streets
Oh yeah, hate is my best friend who's also famous for these feats
I've passed along AIDS with an erection
I'm the reason why the elderly fear for their lives in witness protection
You can call me Blood
You can call me Crip
You can call me Jeffrey Dahmer or Michael Vick
I've taken part in the unjust cruelty of animals
You can find my work in your neighborhood, in literature, or on your favorite TV channel
And in every arsons flame you can find my name
I'm also notorious in this age old drug game
My resume' is extensive
My credentials are crude
I'm the cause of your wife being a widow at home, alone depressed with the blues
I've conquered the world and caused wars
The reason why children go to school, with new bruises and unexplained sores
I've instilled fear and caused undeserved confidence
I'm responsible for the bullet that caused your four year old not to walk again
I've given death penalties and life sentences

I'm the reason why your life is in trenches
I've shattered dreams and robbed futures
I'm the reason why your two year olds in the O.R being prepped for vaginal sutures
I'm the reason why your mother will never speak again, a slice to her throat left her silenced
The reason why your little brother was found in the alley, hollow tips in his head on the day that he was supposed to start college
How could you ever forget me?
These life experiences, should have given you knowledge
Let me re-introduce myself, so you'll always remember
My name is Violence,
And wherever there is greed, hate, envy, or negativity, I'm never too far away, traveling at a close distance behind it

Mirrored Effect

Dick hard
Broad shoulders, folds her under his strength as she gives herself to him, and he takes her
To a place that she believes is love because no man has ever touched her this way
Stroked her gently
Caressed her hair or simply wanted her close
Her mother taught her that she was the reason her daddy coasted out of her life, so she slept with a nightlight in hopes to catch him as he escaped from her dreams
The sunshine of reality stings as she awakens just late enough to miss him
Looking in the mirror, trying to find a glimpse of him in her eyes so she could for once, just lean in and kiss him
But the mirror only showed her what she's always seen, self loathing, and broken particles of herself
And with a mother who was struggling with her own mental health, for this pre-teen there was no help
Just as well as she did every morning she stomped out of the house with hell in her eyes
But this time she cried about her route to school
Predator in the form of her neighbor saw her tears as vulnerability and took this opportunity to make his move
He stopped her and asked why a beautiful girl would feel so sad
With no one else to confide in, she told him stories of an unwanted 12 year old girl with no love from her mom and dad
He grabbed her hand a placed in it a few flowers from his garden, hoping that their roots would birth her trust in him

What she saw as a sweet gesture lit a sparkle in her eyes so he seized the moment and invited her in to his sanctuary of sin
Lead her to the kitchen and sat her down at the table and began to caress her and wipe her tears
Her heart internally cheered at the thought that this man actually cared
But she misread his perversion as compassion
The passion in his actions made her comfortable enough that when he propositioned her, she obliged
It was logical in her mind to comply because she thought she would never experience love, so in comparison to none at all she assumed this was fine
He kissed her cheek and ran his fingers along her spine as he stood behind her at the table
Whispering fable's of forever in her ear as he mentally and physically starts to manipulate her
Her mind said this was ok, but the pain and the blood that leaked from her body screamed "Danger, Danger" as she begged for him to stop
But he would not and in effort to cope with the pain she drifted off into a dream, running in fields with her father
She imagined him strong and mighty as if he was fashioned in the protection of a warrior's armor
But yet again she didnt wake up in time for him to save her from the nightmares of her reality
9 months later she awakened in the hospitals o.r with life being removed from her abdominal cavity, as a safety precaution so that her baby wouldn't contract H.I.V
Thankfully she bore a healthy baby girl but what worried her was the fact that she would never know her daddy
She realized that she could never play the role of father but she vowed to be the best mother that she could be, so that her daughter wouldn't

lose her life trying to find her validity in the word... and it costing her indefinitely...

She already paid that costs and was in no way willing to let her daughter divide the fee...

Voices of the Suicidal

I wonder
If I jump, will there be anyone there to catch me
If I attempt to slit my wrists, will they stop, or stand by and just let me
If I pull the trigger, how soon will they forget me?
Quickly
I imagine almost instantly
Because here in life they don't even value or respect me
They all find ways to disregard, hurt, or neglect me, when I just want someone to love me,
Save me,
Come get me
Rescue me from myself because I too am an enemy
But they're not paying attention
They don't care
So they're not listening
So no...
I won't be showing up for work tomorrow because I've got someplace else to be
But I know it won't be hard for them to find someone else to replace me
And I don't want to go home because I don't want to be abused anymore I don't want daddy to rape me
My hearts been severed, it's like life's been designed to break me
The kids at school call me crazy
With my tattoos and piercings they find reason to berate me
The Heterosexuals antagonize, they bully and tease because they hate me
The Christians are holier than thou, seems everyone wears the judge's robe lately

12 years old and carrying my brother's baby
But it's not my fault, incest runs in my family, it's the way my parents raised me
Black man fit the description of any criminal so cops have all reasons to beat, embarrass and mace me
And before hauling me off for another crime I didn't commit, they spit in my face, call me nigger and taser me
So No...
No more will I be taking
I'd rather them find me in my room and see me hanging
Or a bag over my head asphyxiating
Or submerged in the sea, cold and suffocating
Because I cannot deal
I refuse to exist in a world where pain is all that I feel
Where sunshine is just a mirage in the deserts of hell on a hill
So I'm going to find my way out... in this bottle... in these pills
And maybe I'll get behind the wheel, and along with mine take another life so someone else can know the agony that I feel
They say that misery loves company
That's why I'm taking your joy with me
I've always been the generous type, so I'd like for someone to share in this desolation that I'm living
Knife to this cracker's throat, and if you come any closer you'll just tempt me
To force him to stop calling me Nigger by removing his voice box from his larynx
See you're the same Klan member who threatened to lynch me
And there's that bully who calls me fat, as he punches and kicks me
And there's that black kid who hits me at school because my skin looks different
And there's that perfect person who sends my soul to hell because homosexuality is a sin, says Leviticus

And there's the husband that beats me
And there's that addict mother who gave me away for drugs at the cost of my virginity
And you're the robber, who was caught breaking into my home so you killed my wife and family
And you're the pastor who lured us into molestation using your title, some toys, and candy
And my subconscious is telling me to hold on but I just can't fathom taking anymore... its baffling
So... I say no
No more
I'm going to end it all because I'm tired of this inhumanity
Tired of giving my all just to be robbed of my sanity
Tired of being judged by my shell, my anatomy
I'm tired of being lonely
I'm tired of the apathy
I'm tired of the ridicule
I'm tired of the shame
I'm tired of racism and abuse I'm tired being called names
I'm tired of hunger
I'm tired of pain
I'm tired of hopelessness, I'm tired of hate
Tired of bills and being berated, harassed and abused for my faith
I'm tired of fear; I'm tired of no change
And if I could, I'd do it all again
But it's too late because we can't turn back the hands of time
We can't reload those bullets and undo the damage that these blades have done inside
We can't breathe again to forgive or say goodbye
All we can give is this letter that you've found next to our bodies explaining our turmoil, and the roles that you've played in our suicides

Don't listen when it's too late and suicide notes become their voices

Casual Sex & Self Respect

Wet like
Pre-cum, kisses and cunnilingus
Why are our only lusts for those that involve pussy and penis?
If we focused more of our desires on having some type of self worth and attaining moral achievements, we'll discover that we are so much more than just a physical convenience
Yea of course sex is pleasing
But sex is not the solution when trying to get to know you, because sex always involves at least a party of two
And if sex is all that you're good for to someone else, then what good is that to the soul of you?
Rank high in the sack but diminishing is your value
Real good with your neck, but your mindset is of lesser value
Take wood on your back because you think that somewhere inside of your thighs, he'll discover your value
But I bet if you re-evaluate what you value, you'll realize that you don't value yourself
Auctioning off your body, trying to find a love that you can only offer yourself
This mistreatment and miss-use of others is only a reflection of the behaviors that you've subjected yourself to
How do you expect to gain respect, when you don't even respect you?
Dividing your body up in separate pieces, in separate places, for separate or collective persons
Going to extremes, where people can put wealth in your pockets, but ultimately render you worthless
Because even after emptying their wallets and purses they walk away with your principles and stagnate your purpose
You allow them to rob and degrade, defile you as a person

And you're left searching for the promise in those unwritten vows that we should all make to ourselves
To love, honor and obey, but how can we do that if we've never learned to respect ourselves
To me, there's not enough respect left in casual sex
Casual sex only shows that you're a casualty
Another soul left wounded by the lack of their own self respect... trying to find the cure in other beings and other bodies
But the answer lives internally

Adult Orphan/ Mommy Void

I'm in the land of the lost
Left on deserted roads
Backed up and congested with deserted souls, who all got their own crosses to bear
I'm all alone but yet there's so many of us living... or shall I say existing among the dead here
Worn shoe laces took their places but we're laced up in fear
Akin to when Jesus walked on water, we walk on streets paved in liquefied pains that re-created Frank Oceans of our tears
We made motions of hitchhikers, in hopes that someone will pick us up and hold us near
Take us home and love us dear
But in the process we've gotten the complete opposite
After being picked up, we were beat down and hit with emotional bricks
Kicked out and left wounded
Broken and bruised with pains that have yet to attain a remedy or find soothing
Nurturing arms with strength strong enough to cause these emotional restraints to unloosen
Descended maternal extensions forced us descendants to become reclusive
Shattering beautiful impracticalities because reality is not illusive
But conclusive to the fact that life will lead you to some dim lit locations
Walking in places where abrasions go deeper than skin and your spirit retains lacerations

Sometimes taking you on dark detours to destinations of abandoned roads, where lonely orphan souls are left waiting for someone to love them
Then I look around and I realize that this is the demographic of which I fit in
On this lonely route
Surrounded by a neglected group of children whose parents have departed or simply abandoned them
I'm the son of a dead father and a mother who has discarded him
An of age, derelict, son
Has made me an Adult Orphan
Security's been destroyed because there's no one to fill the mommy void...

Conversation with the Man in the Mirror

I need
To negate these nooses that have been produced and carried out by
fear
It's become painstakingly clear that, that's the reason why we're here
Mirror, mirror
On the wall
It's been my fear of failure that's caused you to fall
Opportunity knocks, but I leave it standing at the door and I avoid its
call
And that's why you've been bound to this perdition
Broken dreams
That planted seeds
And bore the fruits of my affliction
Keeping you from the great that you've been destined to
Destined to be and destined to see
All of your disconnects and downfalls have been products of me
Because I couldn't see that, that would be the cause of my mutilation
and persecution of self
Mirror, mirror I'm no good for you, I'm bad for your health
And that's why you've been slighted
Because of me, your noose has been tightened and you can't breathe
Watching as a guilty by-stander, as you hang and swing, like strange
fruit from trees
Take a look and see
All the trouble I've ignited
I have wronged things that should have been check marked "smiley
faced and righted"
So I'll shed light on it
And the fact is, I've been robbing you

Feeding you poison, instead of feeding your purpose, I've muffled and misguided you
I've hindered your dreams, I've held you back
I've deceived and I've lied to you
I've disguised and devised suicide
Planted bombs within your arms, out of fear, that failure is what the future had laid for you... which leads me back to the mutilation of me
Puncturing holes much deeper when I realize that I've strangled all that you were meant to be
As I shatter surface, I stare at a broken reflection and realize that all of this destruction was caused by me
I've blocked my own blessings by conforming to fear and becoming a slave on the plantation of my mentality
I apologize
And I beg for the person that I see to be set free
And then I realize
The man in the mirror... is me...

Time

If I could manipulate moments, time would never die and I'd live in your love for eternity
I'd marry my future to your forever, even beyond the time that I'm placed six feet under and the gravediggers bury me
There'd be no need to hurry, because if it were up to me, years would become days
And days would become hours and we would spend ours living every moment of every second presently
Disobeying time and the guidelines that ensures that all that begins will have an ending
Just to create a permanent time and space that could never erase, but only guarantee the love in which we've been living
Something so sure and indefinite that it would last long after clocks die and stop watches stop ticking
And our hearts will live blissfully, forever kissing calendars of years whose months have no end
Decades and centuries of evermore that's everlasting, ceaseless- without end
And we will enter into a lifetime of love that will last a lifetime
Who wants to be a millionaire, minus the currency because your love would be the prize and my life line
Autumn, winter, summer and springtime
Living by our own clocks that tick tock to the flow of our heartbeats in sync rhyme
If I could just formulate a formula that could procrastinate or abolish a conclusion
We'd live in a consistent state of continuance, as time becomes disillusioned

Moments will suffer contusions as we live them as long and as frequently as we desire
I'd shatter hour glasses, destroy pendulums and set sundials on fire just to ensure that our time does not expire
Because your love appears to have no limits, it's timeless to me
So if time threatens an end or restrictions, then I guess that it's best, that I loved you
Quickly...

Dignified Death Dealer

Dignified death dealer
To some, he's considered a problem healer but to me, he's simply a stealer of life
A killer made right
A murderer who has M.D attached to his name, so I guess that makes it alright to take away someone's right to live
The life of an unborn child is still the life of a human being
The life of a kid
But yet they are free and able to give a helping hand in the homicide of these individuals and not be considered an accomplice of murder
With occupations nurtured by respect, illness, silent voices, quiet approval and payment
Allowing the voices of these helpless individuals to be left latent, when no one will speak up for them
Their rights have been disregarded like they are not living beings
But every time one kicks, I remember the excitement for the journey of life, and inaudibly screaming
"Please let me live"
Don't count me out of the blessing that is GOD's gift of life
If I could I'd put up a fight, but I'm going through gestation and I'm still developing
And my wants are defenseless against your surgical steels, tools and surgeries
Please mommy don't let them vacuum the life away from me
Don't let them perform the abdominal surgery
They want to kill me chemically but mommy I'm depending on you
If you allow them to hurt me, then you're guilty also
You're a death dealer too
GOD gave my life to you, so you could love and protect me

But here you are taking a part in my murder, playing the role of an accessory
Sitting here with your legs gapped open in stirrups allowing these doctors to dissect me
But I am not a biology project
I'm an unappreciated blessing
Seen as nothing more than a problem to you and a solution to fatten the death dealer's pockets
The doctor enters the room, close the door and lock it, before he performs this procedure sociopathically
As he sucks the life right out of me,
You're crying and you're bleeding
I'm silently depleting
As he walks away with dignity
A medically respected hit-man who has just administered death to me

True Artistry

Dying in illusion
The music misconstrues them and fuses their realities and personalities with that of false alters
Egotistical machinery
Representative of human beings existing through this puppetry
Drones dressed up in make-up and jewelry
Muppets popularizing ignorance and foolery
Soliciting Satan via mass media CDs and TV screens
Spitting bars that make no sense but is sensible to the study of sorcery
Glorifying the enemy while making the King a mockery
Blazing microphones with fire as their tongues burn with blasphemy
Massively serving tragedy through gimmicks dressed so glamorously
This is no longer just music, and it's become deeper than rap, when souls started becoming casualties
Rhyme and verse is in a state of emergency
But I plan to rescue it with a blessing because the saviors present in this poetry
The purpose died when fame became the urgency
Stardom surgically removed the intent of the gift when the gift became the curse and birthed earthly riches
Morale died and pride expired when the only (sense) made dollars and digits
The industry no longer celebrates artistry, only marketing schemes and gimmicks
With the intentions to desensitize society
Kill the conscious being and manufacture a celebrity
Giving them cross-over appeal to go global and brainwash in mass quantities

Booking sold out shows as they perform and pose all the while doing evil works anonymously
And we call them musical geniuses but yet they've misplaced the syncopation of GOD's harmonies...
Without the Creator
The Painter
The Writer
The Savior
There is no True Artistry

Masquerade, Make Me Beautiful

Make me beautiful
Make me nice
Make them love me
Make me right
I'll be your Barbie
Even Ken
With silicones and plastics, I can win
I'll be good
Promote your goods
A walking signpost
Call me billboard
Misplaced confidence in counterfeit cures
Trying to meet the standards, of Elle, Vogue, and Allure
Following the allure
Of this American Standard
Me being an individual is like good humor of banter
I need to fit this mean or mold
What is the cause?
I don't know
Enhance the lesser
Shave the plus
Depreciate my being; hide me behind cosmetic liquids and dust
Make me easy
And breezy like the wind
So when I look at my reflection, I don't recognize who I am
Problem areas marked
With markers on skin
Make me better
I've got to fit in

MAC on the surface
Without it I'm worthless
A sore to the eye like sinuses or pigmentosus
Hide my scars
Past epidermal walls
Cover them until I appear to have no pain at all
Botox injections
Chemical peels
Manufacture my esteem through surgical steels
I'll make a deal
And strip nude of myself
But as long as they love me, I'll find purpose in social wealth
So give me beauty
Or give me death
Living life for vanity or I'll have nothing left
So pick me up
With nips and tucks
Transplant surgeries and liposuck
Reconstruct
My appearance for your approval
Adjust anything that may appear
As weird or unusual
Augmented
Beyond bones and skin
When will they realize that it's GOD, the creator that re-structures the soul within

Murder/Suicide (My Heart's Eulogy)

Today you confirmed my fears
And as the words pierced my ears, I felt it as my heart disintegrated
No physical wounds, but my core was broken and bruised as the truth of your words penetrated, and left bloody... evidence at the scene
And in that split second our love flashed by me, and I saw trouble approaching but I couldn't leave
See I was stuck
And I didn't know how to step out of love so I sat back and watched, as my heart choked, as if oxygen was discontinued by trees
And as I grieve over the loss of my own heart, I can't help but realize that I've committed suicide by allowing this to happen to me
See, I was its sole protector
Should have caged it like Hannibal Lecter
Traveled to Egypt, dug up the dirt, and hid it away like buried treasure
See, these words can't measure or match my pain
These words can't conceal or mask my pain
These words can't capture or trap my pain
These words are only mediocre metaphors of how my sunshine has been outcast by rain
I feel like I'm on my Emo tip
Emote these emotions and you'll see how deeply words can rip
But yet they say
"Sticks and stones may break my bones but words can never hurt me"
Well, maybe they're right because I feel like these words went beyond pain
They left me slain like a homicide victim; they masked up, and murdered me
Then carried me away in a hearse

If you look on the outskirts, you'll see my heart on the inside still bleeding love for you
It has yet to die, that's how you know that it's authentic and true
But, I guess this would have never happened had I shielded myself with more love for me instead of wrapping it all around you
Then, my fort would have been strong enough to bear this catastrophe
If only I had been better prepared, this wouldn't be my heart's eulogy
I've committed suicide
By giving you the power that could murder me

Flawed Fabrications

I
Savored lies that lied upon lips
Plagiarized fairy tale endings of playwrights that only resided upon scripts
I lived in myths that birthed stories of which my happiness could exist
So I could fit into any fit where it was safe for me to dismiss my truth
Further tightening my noose as I choked on fabrications
Forcing them down with libations sweetened by fear
It somehow tasted better to sample a false fantasy than swallow exactly what was really going on here
I made toasts and cheers to living in darkness
Swung upside down by my feet and fright was the harness that held me as I tarnished my being
Diminished 20/20 vision and placed a blur upon clear seeing
In reflected visions appearing was only broken particles of a person
Afraid to scratch the surface out of fear of exposing the imperfectly human side of myself, so I hid away like wanted terrorist
Rebelling against my own truth
Muting my past and all of the agents that's contributed to my outcome
Breaking my own hips to walk in the approved paths of anyone else
I knew not of who I was, so I was unable to recognize the ways to be pleasing and acceptable to myself
Stranger upon my own familiar land
Walking hand and hand with his own dishonesty
"It's all good baby, just continue lying to me, because the truth makes me flawed"
That's what I told myself
After awhile it was no longer hard, so I contorted my existence into any position where I was able to compromise the flip side of a lie

I tried and tried to deny everything that would declare me an imperfection, until I realized that if I don't embrace my shortcomings... then however can I grow?

Dollars and Sense

See, I ain't got to yell and scream for you to see that I'm mean
I spit
Verbal orgasms that pinch nerves, like back spasms, and gives life to wet dreams
Birthing new things with a creativity that the almighty placed within me to speak freedom and bring about change
See I could boast about having chains, diamonds, dollars and change,
But what does that change and who does that help
Remove all that's associated with monetary value and I'd still be considered one who has riches and wealth
Because my assets are stored up in the value of self
So I rebel against this ever so popular, materialistic mindset
Because I know that a dignified man isn't afforded by dollars and cents, but knowledge and sense
And I have enough sense to know that any product that has a price tag doesn't have the power to preserve my soul
That's why I'd rather have Jesus, than silver and gold
So while you're eating diamonds off of a platter, I'm feeding nations, knowledge from a small bowl
Like Jesus fed thousands off of a few loaves
Inspiration from that act alone shows us just how far a gift from the almighty can go
Feed the masses a positive message from your soul instead of materialism through your cash flow
Preserve a life through your pens stroke
Teach them something that's everlasting and deeper than a dick's stroke
Possessions more valuable than Gucci, Louie and Coach
Something bigger and better than Maybachs, Bentleys and Rolls

Because none of these things makes you a better person
They just proved that you've been hoaxed
Hoaxed into believing that your being is made bigger by these things
Coaxed into thinking that your self worth appreciates by these physical trappings that's been glamorized by irresponsible talents on a quest to collect fame
But the fortune doesn't lie in the fame
The fortune's within yourself
When you can stand on your own two feet
Naked of all of the trappings, knowing that you've served your purpose, and in the end the Lord can say "Good Job my child" "You've done well"

Fatherless

Photo albums of still life images weren't enough
Elaborate stories and imaginary scenes that played out similar to his unconscious dreams weren't enough for a little boy growing up without a father figure
He grew tired of his mother's disguised hand written note cards and toys delivered at Christmas
He tired of drawing pictures of the father he never knew
Needed answers to the questions of why his hair was of a less course texture and his skin of a much lighter hue
He wondered, well if my daddy is alive and well... Why doesn't he call?
And if he's really supposed to care, then why doesn't he visit at all
He asks
Doesn't he love me mom?
And her face becomes grim
Doesn't he want to hug me mom?
And she grabs her little boy and nestles him
As liquefied pain excretes from her broken heart and down her face to her chin
She holds him as he vents
"Because I just want to touch him"
I want to know that he is real
I want to feel his skin, and know that he is comprised of flesh, blood, nerve endings and pigment
I want him to know that he has a man child growing up on his own and I'm not some type of cancer that's growing malignant
I want to know that my daddy is not just one of my childlike visions or one of my active imagination's figments
I want to know that his love is someplace waiting, approaching, and looming

I want to know that he's veins, a heart, he's human
Why doesn't he show me his heart, why won't he show me he's human?
His mother hushes him with a gentle finger and whispers
"Your father is all of those things but he doesn't consider you equally the same"
She cupped his chin and looked him in the eyes, as she pulled the cover off the truth that she'd been hiding with a decade of lies
She lifted her housecoat and exposed to her son, her dark hips and thick thighs
"See your daddy is of European descent
First born to a Klansman
So he maliciously took pleasure in my body although he hated me for my skin tone and the fact that you... the nigger child that was growing inside of me, was half black and the product of him"
At that moment, he realized that he had something with his mother that he could never attain from his father to potentially lose
He seen the difference in their genetic characteristics and seen that her love was unconditional and true
Because her love didn't hate
Her Love knew no hues
Her Love had no bearings on physical attributes
Because Love has no preference
Love doesn't choose
Love only Loves
When Love, loves you

Poem Cry

My eyes will no longer cry
Because someone's got to be the poet
Comprised of unwanted and adverse components that makes them unlovable
Someone's got to be unnoticed
That broken structure that's open to malice and hopes that remain hopeless
Someone's got to be those forgotten vessels and veins, that bleeding through pain beyond flesh wounds that remain broken
Those untreated abrasions, those infected and contaminated lacerations of contusions left open
Soaking up the soot of rejection
Something has got to be the reflection of this impoverished heart
The representation of this imperfect product and its malfunctioning parts
The living depiction of this affliction that's been captured by this art
Someone has got to exist in the dark, to reflect its hue accurately
Someone's got to be... the physical form of these words and its pain's potency, to translate this agony in the composition of poetry
Don't want to sound like woe is me, but the fact is "I'm hurting"
I know poetry is often told metaphorically but my body is literally hurting
Internally, my heart is breaking and burning
But my flesh and bones are feeling the effects because there is true pain in my chest where I am physically hurting
Naturally, pain is disturbing
So don't be alarmed if you find my poetry screaming and yearning
My heart's been fragmented so it's only natural to find blood hemorrhaging from my wording

As these verses are emerging from my tongue, I remind myself that
my eyes will no longer cry my heart's agonies
Because my soul weeps through this poetry

Victim of Human Trafficking

Some would consider me to be a rich kid because I come from a wealthy family
A spoiled brat and I must agree
Known to be temperamental when I'm told no, or if my parents disagree
For example; just a few moments previously
My parents wouldn't appease me
So I ranted about how much I hated them and how I longed for a new family
And when they didn't entertain me, I went down to the creek to clear my head, when I stumbled upon a message in a bottle
And it read

Dear Diary,
The "red headed girl" is how they describe me
Innocent eyes
Unexplored thighs, not even standing 5ft
A petite little sweet, ripened cherry pie, appealing to the eye, breast cup about a b
She's only 15
Place the proper bid and you can have her temporarily
What's happening to me?
They're putting me up for sale as if I'm human property
Live Stock
Literally
This wasn't the way it was supposed to be
I just wanted to get away from daddy's drunken beatings and the manhandling... so I ran out into the streets
Then this man approached me
He said he'd protect me and eliminate my worries

He ensured my safety
Promised me jewelry, security, said that he could even make me a celebrity
And just that quickly, I lost my identity
Young American girl about to explore the world, when I'd never even left my city
Currently we travel domestically, so far Chicago, Florida and Philly
During our last trip, I was tied up and placed into a trunk, so I currently have no knowledge of my location or visibility
I hear talks of Italy
Some high paid pedophile is willing to pay top dollar to do some perverted things to me
But I pray that this ends before they ship me
Unlike David and Penny who are now victims of the child porn industry
So many times I've plotted my escape but getting away will only jeopardize the lives of my family
So I suffer through this agony
The sodomy and tongue lashings
The gang rapes, the gun play, the molestation and the battery
I just pray someone finds me
Before this ends tragically
Fearfully signed
A Victim of Human Trafficking…

Apathy

I've ditched my heart
Dumped the remains of my emotions in a dumpster and fled

I left them dead like the rest of me
Opened up life's cookbook and discovered the secret ingredient to this dangerous recipe

Now I'm cookin' up Apathy and serving it no temp
It's vacant just like me, abandoned building, no rent

Look in the mirror and discover my "sixth sense"
"I see dead people" but a grave that's absent

Take your pick, I've ascended or descended beyond this place of concern
No fucks given, and not a care has been earned
But what I've learned is emotional detachment
Separated my interactions with feelings until I became numb, when I once wore my heart upon my sleeve like new fashions

Abandoned the warmth of macramé's, cotton's and other fabrics when I realized that I am not Christ and this is not the passion

So pass me by if you're looking for any type of emotional reaction
You'd probably have better luck with someone who's is certifiably sociopathic

I've lost the understanding of joy, pain and the rest of those feelings that I once practiced

Now I smile when I should be crying and I cry when I should be laughing, possibly a tad bit psychopathic
But when I lapsed into Apathy, I dismembered my sanity and divided it amongst caskets

This could possibly be tragic but I sense no fear
I'm exactly where I want to be, because with the inability to feel, I have no reason to be scared

I simply care not enough for the concept of hurt
So stay away from this malfunctioning product because this is where the most danger lurks

No Ceilings

I see no ceilings
Just success
Stumbling blocks in my way but I'll past the test
With drive and determination, I'll surpass the rest
And that's why I give this my all with every ounce of my being, and not a drop less
The passion of this poet is true, you can see the love spilling from my heart through my chest
But many peoples' passions only go, as far as, the tongue of their flesh
And when they open their mouths, they don't even give you their best
Only words filled with letters but lacking true depth
And that's why I'm going to make it like "The band" minus the rest, Babs, and Elliot Ness
See if I'm the Prince, then it's my Princess
If it were human like a member of my family, I'd probably love it until it was incest
Be it man, woman, or transvest,
I just can't give it up… but I digress
See, these words aren't spoken without substance, because my goal isn't just to impress
So when I speak, I'm giving you all of me, 100% is what I invest
Like throwback greats, just check my ancest
Maya Angelou and Langston Hughes, who've paved the way for the new, now and the next
You can't deny me, the proof is in my performance and the writing of my text
And that's why the devil is trying to destroy my present day because he knows that my future is blessed…
But what GOD has for me, no one can take

While you're sleeping with your eyes open, I'm truly awake
Because great can't wait
Me, I'm more like the V.I.P Pass while you're still standing at the gate
See, I've already swam across the ocean, when you haven't even put your foot in the lake
If you looked in the dictionary, you'd find your face next to procrastinate
But you can associate me with a Snicker Bar "I'm hungry, why wait?"
When you sit on your gifts, you suffocate a blessing and for someone it may be too late
See, this gift to me is as good as ice cream and birthday cake
As exciting as first dates
An overwhelming feeling like the first climax when a teen learns to masturbate
So engulfed in my gift that I'm writing in my sleep, what can I say...
its fate
Before GOD gave me this gift, he marinated it in blessings, then placed it upon my plate
And now I want to share it with you
And trust, I'm going to make it do what it do
Write lines until gray skies turn blue
Penning words until the homeless have shoes
Speaking power until disease ridden individuals are like new
It may seem impossible but there's no limit or no ceilings when GOD has called upon you

12

If I could, I'd reach out and catch your last 12 breaths and breathe them back into your body
And your heart will start beating and the aches will stop hurting
Just long enough for me to say that I love you 12 more times
Kiss you on your cheek and watch you spread 12 more smiles
And we'd journey 12 more miles and make 12 more moments
Stretching and divvying up the seconds, however we choose to, because that time would be of the essence, precious, and of our own ownership
And I'd loan you 12 more limbs 10 fingers and 2 arms just to give you 12 more hugs
So snug and so close that there'd be no space in between us
Barely leaving room for Jesus because I'd hold on so tight that no one could ever take you away, that way you could never leave us
And life would feed us 12 more meals that we could dine on for 12 more eternities
Rebirth life in you to prove that I exist through true maternity because without you I'll continue dying for 24 hrs 7 days and 12 more months
If I had a genie that would grant me 3 wishes I'd use 1 to ask for 10 more which would leave me 12 more wants
And all of them would be you
All that I want is you
12 more phone calls just to hear your voice on the other end saying "nephew I love you"
I'd reincarnate all that you were, so great and held is such high regard, that I'd put you up on 12 different pedestals
My grand champion worthy of the bronze silver and 12 golden medals
I'd bring you daisies and rose petals because Aunt Betty always says "don't wait and bring me flowers once I've already died"

*So I'd bring you 12 different bouquets of 12 different roses with 12
different notes that all express that I need you to survive
And I'd buy 12 different shares of stock in your stock
Purchase 12 different time devices and there be everlasting moments
on each clock
Because when your time stopped, so did my heart
So Ann, if you can
Give me 12 more breaths so we can both breathe again*

Clever

You can't see stars until your mind frame evolves, see you think too little
But when I speak, they're like "put this man on ice, he's hot, he needs a Popsicle"
Trying to implore me with your words, when the most you do is bore me
Catch me getting Z's, hit the snooze button, and hear me snoring
Step your mind frame and your pen game up
Life is so much bigger than fancy clothes, expensive cars and all of the bitches you've fucked
Maybe dick you should suck, because I'm tired of hearing you talking
Pointless words into air like a big dog with muted barking
So your words will never bite, or even pierce me
Someone once asked what good are these words if no one hears me?
So now my heart has been captured and manifested lyrically, and poured out upon those who want to listen
Like the most important meal of the day, I'm the one you should not be missin'
Knowledge is power
Pour yourself a big bowl, when you sit down for breakfast in your kitchen, so you can stay abreast upon what's crucial and important in our realm
I've always heard that an idle mind is the devil's playground
So if you want to stand on greater grounds and live where true beauties bound, then we've got to keep our minds sharp
These demons will try to take all that they can from us
But they can't change what we know to be true, nor what lives in our hearts

*See the material and the superficial shall fade, but the power in
knowledge lasts forever
Re-evaluate and realize what's important in life, but until then
I think your silence will be the only words that I've heard from you
and thought... hmm...
"Clever"*

Weaponry of Words

You should be careful of the way that you handle people
Because you don't know what some people can handle
See, something that seems to be simple as weightless, insubstantial words could dismast and dismantle
And burn like candles to the soul of an individual
And you may never know it because all pains are not displayed upon the canvas of the physical
And you realize that when you're leaning over a box, to just a body and there's no soul among the residuals
At the funeral standing by listening as loved ones sniffle, as they wipe their grief stricken souls with a tissue
Then you grasp the fact that words are not just letters and syllables
But they can be as fatal as lethal injections when you're not careful of what your tongue is capable

Never Love Again

Forgotten letters

Haiku poems and words on pages

Weren't just words on pages, but documentations of my heart rediscovering love's destination

I had forgotten the steps and paces that had always landed my heart in those broken places before I found you

I thought that you were love's personification but, then you left too

And unintentionally bruised meagerly healed wounds of a heart that was already broken

Just a few simple words tore it apart and ripped its sutures wide open

And again I found myself hopeless and loveless

Feeling like I died 100 deaths

Like you tore out my heart, broke it and stuck it back in my chest... to continue bleeding love for you

I guess that I'm not the guy to trust with stocks and bonds because I always choose the wrong thing to invest into

All of my investments seem to turn out as non-profitable

I guess we can all say that I'm really bad at choosing

I just know that I am sick, and tired, of losing

Tired of the ones that I love most, simply perusing through parts of my life, and then tossing me aside like a book that doesn't deserve to be read

I'm tired of breathing air everyday and still feeling as if I'm dead

I'm tired of these doubts and insecurities running through my head

I'm tired of relationships only being good enough for just a fuck, I want passion, no more lust in my bed

"Because I just want to be loved"

"I just want to be loved"

"No quickies instead"

Fast foods can't nurture what I'm missin'
I'm yearning for nutrition
If love isn't what you're serving, then take your soups out of my kitchen
You've been denied access and permission to be here
Deborah Cox said that "Nobody's Supposed to be here" So why did I let you in
I was a fool to believe that love would truly happen, but this time I've learned my lesson
In the words of Janet Jackson,
"Because I will never fall in love with you again"
But I guess that I can't because I already am
But we can refer to you as the finale of my heart,
Roll the credits on love because for me, this is the end
Call "cut" because after this ends, I'll take a bow and I'll make a vow
and I promise to myself that I will never love again

The Realest Shit I've Ever Wrote

She said baby "This the realest shit I ever wrote"
With every stroke she scribed rhymes and notes, signed, sealed, and delivered on my tongue... in cum
As her ink runs down my face I enjoy her poetic box of poetry
Three line haikus followed by sonnets and then she free writes all over me
As I explore the depth between her lines and her thighs, my fingers become intertwined with her gifts
This turns into a collaboration piece as we spit
I drift into passionate moments of poetry and bestow my love upon her clit
As my fingers and tongue explore pages of labia and lips, I take sips of her wetness and I like the way it tastes
Always had a hunger for knowledge she quenches my thirst, as she feeds my face, and creates beautiful art using me as her muse
With me, she shares that delectable juice
See, every time I taste her, she gets inspired to write
Her mouth opens wide as her pussy recites climatic cadences upon my tongue cleverly disguised as her mic
Damn she's tight, lyrically slick, wet, and deep
She tries to speak, making mentions of a mute but I know when she's pleased because her body communicates as she trembles and she buckles at the knees
With no table manners, I devour every ounce of passion, slurping, as I dine on her delivery
Massaging, kissing, touching, licking, and thumbing through pages of ink stained wetness
I succumb to her harmonic blessing
Dripping delicious dances, draining her drenched decadence

*Eruptions of erotic expressions expressed in exact elegance
Fulfilling fruitful fantasies, as I taste the fluid in her deepest
composition of poetry, one of which her body has always hoped
Serving me samples of ecstasy as I swallow its nutrients down my
throat
As her ink explodes, she pulls me close, then signs her signature upon
my piece and says
"Baby... This the realest shit I've ever wrote"*

Physically Trapped In Physical Traps

She's become complacent with the normality of being hit
But being abused is not normal shit
"I mean" it may be common but it's never ok
But the money he throws her way softens the blow that just blackened her eye yesterday
And just a week prior, he broke her nose and bruised her ribs
The abuse is so extensive that she can no longer bear kids
But the presidents printed on the currency, helps her to turn the other cheek for another day
As long as the Prada and Fendi continues to come her way she'll continue to lay with death
Until he finally takes her last breath and it'll be too late to say that enough is enough because I value my life
And I refuse to be the victim of your blunder and blight
But for tonight, she'll settle for more abuse, because she knows that Franklins and Grants will be there for her in the morning
Moral values and self worth to her, has always been foreign so she lives comfortable with this life
Until one day, she wakes up staring down the barrel of a 45 and her soul has taken flight
All of these materialistic and physical trappings gave her tunneled vision
It blurred her sight
She was on a quest to get it
But just didn't know that it would cost her ...her life

Casualty of Love

Eyes swollen
Heart broken
And I'm hoping that somehow I'll find the strength to go on
Bury my pain at the bottom of this sea of tears
I look into your eyes, as we cry together, relinquishing our hurt and fears amongst the earth
Our bodies join together for one last embrace and I can feel your heartbeat...
I can feel its hurt
As your body trembles in my arms, my heart sings a song that says that I will always love you
Neither of us wants to let go but we both know that it's something that we must do
Although it's evident that we're meant to be because our souls speak even when our tongues are non-verbal
Your love is herbal to me
All natural
Unconditioned and pure
Indefinite
Guaranteed
Always and for sure
As I kiss those lips, I become lost in your
Beautiful soul
But I like this kind of displacement because being lost in you feels like home
This is where I want to be
This is where I belong
See, living life without you would equate to me living life too long

Being devoid of you is like dying a thousand tragic deaths and being re-birthed in the devil's arms
Leaving me
Undoubtedly
A casualty of love
See, you can deny O.J's guilt but there's no refuting yours because when you open up your palm,
the evidence of my D.N.A's in your gloves
My heart's in your hands
Still bleeding love

Selfless Couture

Ingested poison in the form of a camouflaged cure
Adopting labels and name brands to reflect value that was never present before
So they've placed their stock in markets that targets the pockets of those who don't know how to love themselves
Just to buy a little bit of confidence
Broadening their arrogance and cockiness manufactured by these famed images when these individuals don't even know who they are yet
Nursing their wounds and scars with price tags but the simple value of self should be the first priority of any budget
But love lived in the fabric of materialistic magic and afforded the admiration of those who couldn't afford it or simply didn't need it
Unlike these beings who fiend it because it's a must to keep their stock up
Hustling for the mark up because there's no value in the sale
Searching for self worth in retail to unveil it upon community stages of attention
Glistening in the opportune spotlight to show off their riches
As onlookers pity their figments of true value
Salutations are made by blatant displays of that which they value, alluding to the fact that they have yet to learn their worth
Scraping this earth for a little piece of something to share with the world so that someone can love them
The fact that they are already loved is unbeknownst to them, because they've yet to discover and understand the beauty within
Trying to find their worth in the significance of monetary earnings
But the beauty that is simply you, is more valuable than any physical furnishings

Life Support

I was birthed on life support
Was supposed to be the supporter of my own life but somehow I still can't breathe
Reason being because I'm more like the strangler with a bag over my head suffocating and taking my own life
Desist and disease
Halted my breathing and stopping my own heart
Tearing my lungs from my thoracic cavity and ripping them apart
See, I was supposed to be the lead and supporting actor in the presentation of my existence but somehow I snatched the role from myself
Re-wrote the script and became the antagonist
See, Murder's what he wrote for himself
Each time he questioned his abilities,
Each time he fell victim to his insecurities and allowed his impurities to impoverish his self worth
Each time he stomped and kicked himself while he was already laying face down in the dirt
See, I've rebuilt and re-birthed a life that GOD didn't foresee for me
Created an imaginary world of dreams because I couldn't embrace my reality
Or maybe I was scared that I'd be defeated, or I just didn't know how to prevail
But how can you win a battle when you refuse to step into the battlefield,
so automatically you've failed
All the while creating this beautiful imagery
With paints and oils that would convey peace, victory and tranquility but somehow the canvas is still diminishing

On legs too weak to stand,
On faith weakened because the superior half of his anatomy has let go of the Lord's hand
A lost soul
Lost in this lost land
Barely moving, with no improvement and slowly drowning in quick sand

Trying to coexist in a world of which I don't exist
Disproportionate portions of a person shattered all across this existence
Differed subsistence
Auditioned to be myself but derision deterred the ambition of livin
Mission of those so persistent upon hate
Quick to serve your definition of diluted love because the stake is sharp enough to leave one perforated
Subjugated to being wanted, so as long as someone would have me I'd let them take me in fractions
Aware of the infraction that I was bringing upon myself
Compromising pieces of me to be fully accepted by somebody else' standards
Looking for me in the darkness of this conformity and I'm screaming "I can't find you"
Reaching my hands in front of me and I identify familiarity but "I still don't recognize you"
I tried to but there's too many foreign components that's been added
Tried to examine the original labels but the merchandise can't be determined because the damage pierced beyond the package
So for a moment I could only imagine me
Then I see pictures and graphics of the evidence of what I used to be, and in the distance I hear people screaming "Mysfit we miss you"
Resembling the same internalized lines that I've cried for this lost boy within "Mysfit I miss you too"
And for running away I can't blame you
I sold out your being to entities that would only entertain you, remastered and manufactured instead of accepting you as an original
De-escalated your value to give them an altered rendition

Hung upon a cross, subjected suicide by sacrificing myself as crucifixion
In an effort to bleed me of my abnormalities and impracticalities, I sought redemption for my afflictions in everyone opinions and everyone's approval except my own
Was influenced by everyone's decisions and happiness because my happiness was contingent upon everyone's, except my own
Partook in my metaphorical murder and buried my remains hoping that no one else would ever know
Stereotypes and pre-written death sentences ruptured my soul
And they wonder why he calls himself a lost boy
Because, he's been dead and gone a long time ago but yet his body still roams
So Lord I want you to just "swing low sweet chariot, coming for to carry me home"
"Swing low, sweet chariot, coming for to carry me"
HOME

I Am A Black Man

I am a black man
Projected to be the very last man to make a positive change
At best, he'll learn how to dribble a ball but he'll never use his brain
So let him play sports, he's good enough to entertain
Besides that, the most he'll ever be is some hoodlum rapper or the leader of a street gang
Stealing old ladies purses and robbing jewelry stores for their valuables, diamond rings and rope chains
Behind bars for perpetuating murder or the distribution of heroin and crack-cocaine
Deadbeat dad who walks around with his pants off of his ass, neglecting his kids and leaving them for the women or the state to raise
They've prejudged me as trash before giving me a chance; they've already thrown me away
Because I am a black man
And because I am a black man, I know that we can up-stand taller than that negative image that the media paints
Live larger than that illegitimate stigma that society thinks that we are a hazardous liability instead of an asset to change
We are all individuals
Designed by the creator, one of a kind piece originals
So no matter what they perceive as dismal, we still resemble what's great
As long as we have the breath of the almighty in our lungs and the blood of freedom fighters in our veins
See, when opposition's in our faces that pushes us to fight harder
In hindsight of the odds we've become, social workers, teachers, psychologists and lawyers,

Whether you choose, or choose not to support us
Any man with a penis can be a daddy but we're men with passion, purpose, power, and principals so we pride ourselves on being good fathers
Who honor our reflection and respect our women
Evolving from slavery, broken homes, abuse and addiction
And we've made it our mission in life to not be conditioned by those malnutritioned traditions of our past
So when anyone says that we can't, we'll contradict them with the Obama campaign slogan "yes we can"
And go on to be great artists, writers and poets, be it with pens, paints or scalpels, we're still doctors with gifted hands
Creating beautiful movements like Black Panthers, Alvin Ailey and Freedom Fighters, no matter our motions, there's a distinct power in our dance
So whenever they attack my flesh, I will stand tall because I am a strong individual
And I just happen to be a black man
Who will not allow anyone to validate or condemn me due to my complexion but only for what I stand for and what I represent
So if you choose to love me or hate me, let it be for whom I am internally, not the color of my skin
Because that's not all that I am
Look beyond what your eyes can see
And you'll see that there's so much more to me, than the fact that I am a black man

For You

I was fine before I met you
Love for me was always one of those things, that I never pressed the issue
And I could go on throughout my day without wanting to kiss you
But now when you're gone too long, I feel like I'm going crazy because I miss you
And I'm not cured until I'm with you
Like a drug to a patient, your presence is medicinal
But for me, this is atypical because I'm starting to act like a fiend for you
I think I'm addicted all of a sudden, I've developed this need for you
Would travel the world and the seven seas for you
Would fight a giant even if I got beat down to my knees for you
Like Trina said "I've got a thing for you"
Would trade the world and all its things for you
My heart beats for you
Fuck a respirator; if I could, I'd breath for you
Ask for the moon and stars and that's what I'd retrieve for you
If in your way, I'd move the mountains and trees for you
This is no pun intended; I'm playing for keeps, for you
No time for games, I'm willing to wear a ring for you
Prayed to the high heavens and King of Kings for you
I'm like glaucoma with a supplemental need for you
But if ever I have to need for you
My heart will forever bleed for you
And I'll be down on bended knees for you
Indeed for you

Rolling Stone/ You Owe Me

("Papa was a rolling stone, wherever he laid his hat was his home and when he died... all he left was a loan")
I reserve the fucking right to dislike you even in death
Wounds remain open from the terror that you've left upon my existence
Little boy still cringes as mentally he watches and listens to his mother cry as that man that she once loved beat her percussions
She'd look into my innocent eyes and saw the guy who was always beating her like percussions
And I paid the consequences and repercussions for your actions
All the while you were out living the life of an alcoholic and addict
Manic Depressive, Bipolar, bullshit excuses
I guess it's supposed to excuse the fact that when you weren't raising hell in our home, you were out being a family man to any family except your own
A great father figure to any fatherless child, you were there for us all... except your own
And I was left to grow up in a divided home, with a brother and mother whom I felt didn't like me because of you
My brother left because he was also a victim of the abuse and my mother became distant, there was no one for me to talk to
A stranger in a family where no one knew me
Outcasted in my own home
And eventually when you were done playing hero, to these women and their children, the wind would blow you back to us
Returning to your role as our villain
But my mother wasn't willing to allow you to kill her so she attempted herself, and chugged down a bottle of prescriptions

I always envisioned that she'd given you so much as a wife, that's why GOD didn't to let you take her life ... So he brought her back to me
And we stayed on the run from you, but you had already robbed her emotionally
So in essence you still took her away
I once heard somebody say
"Sometimes I feel like a motherless child"
It's almost as if I watched her fade away
Short jail bids and restraining orders briefly kept you away
My mother prepared for life as a divorce' but you manipulated the fact that I wanted a family and used me as a pawn to lead you back to her love
But soon you'd come to discover there was nothing left to what was
She was done with excreting blood, and hiding bruises and black eyes
She decided that she wasn't going to take any more and took the measures to extricate you from her life But
I still wanted a father... so how dare you die... Kevin?
I guess that's why you always taught me to call you by your first name because you never had intentions of being any father of mine...
KEVIN!!!
A little boy, just about eleven and you stripped me of the emotional connections of family
You've murdered them emotionally and now I feel like an orphan amongst family
You owe me
Left me the shell of their anatomies but shattered them at the place where they were supposed to love whole hearted and affectionately
You owe me
Left me to live my entire life without a father and my experiences with you accompanies bad memories
You owe me
A mother, a brother, a father a family

GOD let you borrow these people and you haven't made good on your loan
You owe blood of their blood, flesh of their flesh, and bone of their bone
You owe me the most important portion of matter from the pieces of life in which you've stole
Or maybe I owe it to myself to rebuild a relationship with the hearts of these distant individuals that I love, on my own
I can't rely on you to do it because
"Papa was a rolling stone, wherever he laid his hat was his home"
"And when he died... all he left, was a loan"

Suicide Smiles

I am in a very dark place
I just choose to keep the porch lights on
Beautiful frame for the image yet the picture is dead and gone
No life existing beyond the skin of my flesh, there's death beyond my bones
Dead man walking
Mobile headstone... that creeks each time cheeks expand west to east, careful not to expose that I am a walking decedent
Calculate the calculations correctly and others will assume you're living just because they see you smiling and breathing
But they don't know that my soul has been suffocated simply because my heart is still beating
And bleeding just enough to sustain my veins, as I walk around in this temple housing death
Body of a mausoleum
Prayers of a resurrect
Shun these mental death threats but I don't know if I can ward them off any longer
Sanity's slipping away as the voices of murderous, sweet nothings getting stronger
From the outside, the porch lights appear to smile bright but frequent implosions caused its residence to become gravely somber
Holy war waged on my own soul and soil, back away, I'm a suicide...bomber

I wonder how much longer I will deceive the world, as I slowly die, behind the painted lies, of suicide smiles...

Abominable

"My stuff is the anonymous ripped off treasure of the year"
Don't come this way looking for love because there ain't none here
Don't slip up and fall in love with me because what I bleed is below zero and it's slicker than ice sheets, call me cold blooded
The shit that I've been through left me cold hearted, and flame retardant
Kanye West type heartless
With a lack of warmth and a diagnosis of emotional retardation
I have no sense of compassion and me giving a fuck is on permanent vacation to no man's land
So all that love that you've been spitting to me, you can take it, swallow it, let it digest and blow it out your ass because it don't mean shit to me
Yea, I'm gonna tell you why I'm mad
The word, love, has become a fad, the popular thing to do at the moment
But why use the word if you can't afford the actions to own it
And I won't finance bullshit
I ain't even gonna check your credit, and fuck your references
You love me?
Please can all that rhetoric and put it on the market to sell to the next gullible motherfucking impulse buyer
Maybe you should've caught me a few years ago when my heart wasn't so resistant to the fire
Back then, I probably would've listened to your sales pitch but now it's all false advertisement, so to me you're a liar
But if you really want something to do with your love then why don't you pack it up, take it to church and sing it on the choir
The almighty could probably use it more than me

I hear that he loves unconditionally
Sometimes I wonder if that even applies to me
True love seems to be an impossibility
But if you'd like to act on this love that you speak of then why don't you get on your knees...
Remove your unmentionables and show me just how deep
Nope... cuddling won't be necessary, just grab your shit when you're done because I'm accustomed to watching love leave
See, I told you that I bleed below zero degrees Celsius
Compared to me, Antarctica's hot when its climate's at its healthiest, call me glacial
Could give a fuck about your heart, your feelings, or your thoughts, what do I care call me hateful
Because I am now nothing more than just the body of a warm blooded man who's let his heart die in an igloo
Trying so much to adjust to the ways of this cold hearted winter wonderland that I'm becoming a Snowman...
ABOMINABLE

Independently Dependent Upon Assistance

With no wisdom or foresight of tomorrow, they've produced today's carbon copies of their past
Shameful beings
Flying on demoralized broken wings to the highest point of their lowest expectations
Ambitions out of gas because they've reached the peak of their success with half of a high school education
Dreams never reached incubation
See, they died in the hands of discouraging parenting, bad examples and a lack of validation
A lack of positive reinforcements and a lack of communication
Finding comfort in minimalism becomes their motivation to sit back and do nothing for themselves except waiting around to collect government assistance
Direct payments for welfare recipients and food stamps for instance
Their feats of responsibility are printed on a card called independence
But the dependence upon another source refutes that definition
Maybe it should be called the card of dependency
The card of despondency
A get out of jail free... pass for those who thrive off of laziness and irresponsibility
Crippling the growth of individuals by perpetuating their feelings of inadequacy
Adamantly they deny their own abilities to be meagerly cared for by the tax payer's dollars
Quick to claim the title of adult but yet they rely on the state to be their provider
When the government is only supplying the water that feeds the seed planted by those individuals that taught them not to reach

Suffocating the life out of their ambition which forces them not to dream

Treating them like baby cows keeping them bound so they will not roam and they will not grow, leaving their muscles and strength weak like cattle or veal meat

But unlike veal this is no delicacy

It should not be handled delicately

Grown folks who are completely capable and able to care for themselves should not be addicted to the system and my gross wages should not be their dependency

How can someone else be reliant upon my income when sometimes I can't even depend on my salary?

But I guess if the government continues to dish it then that's what they'll take

And the tax payers will be left to raise the families of an uninspired society, as if our tax dollars can fix the defects of bad parenting

Murder Ain't Funny But We Do Love To Laugh

Murder aint funny but we do love to laugh
Echoes and broad casts of hearty snickers linger
Humiliation, jokes, long stares and pointed fingers objectify flaws and imperfection
Detection of difference, subject for ridicule
What may be fun for one, could break the souls of few as you are so perversely entertained
Souls are slain at the expense of one's amusement
Bruising confidences and as we take pleasure in the crescendos of a chuckles delusion
Blue print of broken spirits outlined in the blood stains of hearts contusions
Intangible nooses realized at the loss of a smile
Compromising someone else's joy for the pleasures of ours, as we smear blood across our faces
Licking our chops and tasting death upon our lips
They're drenched in guilt
Witnesses to a bloodbath this is mass murder, accomplice to the culprit called our tongues
We let harsh, brash words freely run away from them, and use verbal expressions as weapons
Efforts to lessen another's joy
Avoiding praises to perpetuate pain
Destroying smiles and sustaining hate, that simply obliterates life
Bright lights of glee slowly fade and begin to darken in the distance as ears listen and deliver messages that incinerates the spirit
Mirrored images of our aches recreated upon another's soul
Publicly writing untold stories of our own demons, trying to appease them by teasing others

Smothering our own hurt by breathing life into another individuals insecurities
Finding comedy in the same things that are secretly killing us... thus Murder aint funny, yet we do love to laugh
We stash our fears within the fears and frowns of other faces
Their sadness encases our feelings of inferiority, hidden behind our humor
Laughter is supposed to be good for the soul but when it's malicious it becomes as lethal as malignant tumors
A cancer of laughter if you will, that's captured and spread through evil smiles
Traveling miles and miles through the body until ones spirit is affected
Deflecting our own disease by infecting others with our venomous invalidity
Sickened mentality, were slow to share the wealth but quick to share the misery
The harm in our decision is a desperate effort to hide the horrors in our flaw
Our small minds are unable to grasp the laws of imperfection, that of which makes us human, because human is not good enough
So we rush to the judgments that defaults us as perfect models
Shattering souls like volume and sound waves to glass bottles
Watching as our words dig hollow graves, as if we were unaware that life and death is in the power of the things we say
Stealing the joy of others because we've yet to find our own so we use crude, evil comments to take other peoples smiles away
Temporarily we wear them upon our face chuckling as their happiness, has gone and come to pass
But murder aint funny... so why do we love to laugh?

No Peace in Quiet

This silence is screaming and screeching through my head
Compromising my sanity, my mental is no safe haven but a war zone instead
Echoes of my misery is all that I hear in this silence
I can't escape this
It's my life
My turmoil
There's no peace in this quiet
It's more like violence to me
Someone please blast the music to eliminate my deep thinking
Or cause a ruckus so that the voices in my head won't be the only ones that I hear screaming
See, I've been dreaming about rediscovering my peace
But lately that's been more like a fantasy
Seems like Peter Pan and Never-Never land would be a more tangible reality
What was once known to propose some type of tranquility has only offered me chaos in this quiet
There's mayhem in my mind deep inside there's a riot
Mute this silence because the noise is killing me
Can you hear it?
Come here and listen closely, there's anarchy
Glass shattering, voices screaming loud and disorderly
These external sounds of nothingness is like assault and battery
Robbing me of my rational and only affording my insanity
So if you can
Please!
Please stop the insanity
Because this silence is chastising, abusing, and mistreating me

Beating against my eardrum and leaving me in misery
Keeping me in this place, where depression visits frequently
Anguish and despair strikes, as the tears flow repeatedly
Bounding me to heartache and caged by despondency
If only someone could... please come talk to me
Whisper in my ear for awhile, so this silence won't continuously haunt me, and wear me down
Just as long as you're not quiet
Because there's no therapy or peace in these silent sounds

Love Undefined By Personal Definition

Why do people use the word love so loosely?
Passing it out like condoms at the free clinic
Don't take them if you don't need them and don't say it if you don't mean it
See, she wanted him to love her
And even though he said he did, he loved nothing more than the way that her curves sat out in the perfect positions and perfect places
He loved the way she'd bow her head and fall to her knees for him, as if she were praying to GOD for his mercy and his graces
He loved the way she'd go the extra mile, green if need be, just to see him happy and in amazement
But he didn't love her
He loved her in the way that his daddy loved his mother
Loveless before she left
Loved her, unlike the way she wanted her father to... the one who she has never met
Loved her in only ways that her uncle did, when she was six years old, laying on her back
He loved her long, far, away, deep, and from a distance
Loved her without passion that of which perverted her uncle's kisses
But yet he holds on to her heart and possesses her existence
All the while possessing her love but he never loved her beyond her clitoris
See... the way he loved on her, he also loved on other women
The way he loved on her, he also loved men and children
The way he loved on her was numb and without feeling
His love was paralyzed for the most part until he showed her his heart
Cold, hard, hurt, sick, and relentless

And engorged with that same bruised blood that bruised her when he loved her with his fist
The only way he knew to show passion came in the form of violence instead of a simple kiss
The only way he knew to spread love was to shed his clothing and share his dick
But he never
Learned to share
His heart
If love wasn't connected to a physical connection, then no love is what she got
So she continued yearning, and longing for the love of him, hoping that one day it'd be so true that it'd flow blue through her blood stream
She realized that this type of love, was loveless, theory of her doctor, proven in the form of H.I.V
His love had only moved her closer to an Acquired Immunodeficiency Syndrome
His love was all that she lived for but at the cost of her life she would have much rather been left alone
Blind, deaf, dumb, and numb to a love that she had been waiting for, be he had never sent it
She realized that all those times that he said that he loved her; he could have never truly meant it
So now she sees her life as a testimony and uses her story as an instrument
Passing out condoms and sharing the gift of that devastating news that she found in the free clinic
See, anyone can say that they love you
But the question is
Can you live with their definition?

Intellectual Whore

I'm a whore for your intellect
Like a harlot for your time
I appreciate your body, but I'm a nympho for your mind
When your tongue speaks its brilliance, I open wide so I can taste it
Delving into the mucous of your mental even the sweetest kiss can't erase this cause I'm an addict for your brain
It's like I'm a junkie and your mind's my cocaine
On a high whenever I'm with you like it's been injected in my veins
And the reaction I can't explain
But I think that we should have brain sex
Like fucking hard and making it rain sex
Like I ain't done until the neighbors know our names sex
I'm just a fucking fiend for your mental
Make love to my mind and leave your DNA on my dentals
You make me climax without even stimulating my physical
And that's why I like to copulate on your endowment
I have an open mind so you can plow it
I'm masturbating with your mental so when it comes raining down I want to shower in it
See, there's power in it
Knowledge is power so when you feed me I'm devouring it
Catch and swallowing it
Nourishing myself with the nutrients of my intellectual
Feeding my needs in ways other than sexual
Yea, your body is beautiful but minus a brain I'd long for something more
See, I'm more attracted to your mental
Guess that makes me an intellectual whore...

The Other Slavery

We're living in a dictatorship
That forces one to break their hips to walk in the path of social ideologies
The land of the free...
Compromised by stereotypes, stigmas and boundaries
Packaging labels are made for packages, and boxes are like cages, which is another representation of slavery
Freedom hanging in our faces but it's only attainable, when we conform to becoming whom they tell us, it's ok for us to be
Pursue your own identity and you're labeled as a threat, a weirdo, or one who's lacking suitable mental capacity
Back in the day, they'd lock you away in facilities when you chose to no longer be a puppet operated by Geppetto's string
Those same things are happening today but not so blatant or done so literally
But rebelling against a trained state of mind classifies you as crazy, simply for being aware or having your own way of thinking
I guess individuality is only acceptable when you're a living piece of machinery; achieving only that of which you've been programmed previously
By the way, there'd be no surprise, when a human scanning app is added to I-pad; since we're being branded and implanted with serial numbers and bar codes to recognize our identities
Although they may be used to track and find me, no numbers or labels can define me
A life forced to serve in servitude, is illegal, isn't it?... something like human trafficking

But instead of caging a physical being, you cage life by placing shackles and restrictions upon personality, principalities and spirituality
What type of living is life worth when you're denied the right to be free?
That's what America's supposed to represent right? Then where's the opportunity for one to simply be
In 1865, the law was abolished that denied a person's liberty
But yet in 2013, even I know why the caged bird sings...
I guess one doesn't have to be in physical captivity to still find themselves in slavery...

Price Tags

I hoarded heaviness in my heart
Tried to deny the fact that there was a hole in me
Reached in and discovered a deep abyss of nothingness, except price tags for pain
Transactions approved, upon the dotted line, life signed my name for preordered problematic products
From my tears ducts I expressed complaints
Faint happiness exchanged for a miserable existence
Abuse, lack of love, empty self worth and no budget to afford joys prescription
Revisited my past, looked around and asked
"Where the fuck is my father?"
Absent from the roll call unless he was beating my mother, or hurting my brother
All of which funded the price tags for hate
A growing distaste amongst loved ones, when love should only taste like GOD's grace
I vacated the premises of promises, in return for faith in the worse case; to waive price tags for disappointment
Trust issues disjointed friendships and relationships
And replacements were price tags for lonesome
Phoned home to contact the kid in me, just to let him know that no one really wants him
Not even me
Receipt read declined
No funds available
But yet I could afford my own insufficiency
Called this place home but yet there were no price tags for equity

Indebted to self, a cost that was never fiscal but stressed emotionally, which bred price tags for bad kidneys
Pill consumption and heavy drinking
Aborted logic and fucked thinking, by taking caution and throwing it to the wind
Could only understand reckless living
No room for reasoning or concerns of kin
Price tags for isolation
Brief anticipation
Found acceptance in one individual and fell in love
Misconstrued being wanted, by the closeness of a distant fuck
Enough was enough; I tired of the trend and price tags for of rejection
Paired with internalized terror were the makings of a deadly weapon
In the form of price tags for prescriptions... mixed them with a longing for freedom and desperation
Suicide was the attempted price tag for emancipation
But only afforded was a brief vacation
And in no time I was back shopping in marketplaces for love
Discovered and realized that I am not good enough, which pointed out my price tags for sin
So hell-bent on the cost of my imperfections and me being who I am, denied me the kingdom and I won't be allowed in
Wasted price tags on pointless breaths expelled from lungs of a dead man walking
Price tags of a living zombie, that doesn't rebel against death but instead against life
Price tags unfunded by those, who are supposed to love in spite
I continue to swipe strips of my life to make the difference and pay the price
But the message still reads
Insufficient Funds
Insufficient Funds

Insufficient Funds

Then I realize that no matter how much I have stored up in my closet full of sorry, that I'll never be good enough to afford to make this right...

Motionless Tears

Motionless tears
They sit upon the cusp of fears
From mommies and daddies that told little black boys that it's not ok
for a man to cry... unless he's a sissy
So he bottles it up
And you wonder why he's angry
He's frustrated he breaks shit
Trying to find a way to release this pent up aggression
The wrong type of pressure can force him to snap at any second,
because tainted; society's conscious parents told him that it was
wrong for him to be human
And since robots can't be birthed, they built one
They oiled his joints with rage and killed all of his future relationships,
by robbing him of rights to be able to express himself
Forcing his temper to turn him into a constant monster in the public
eye as he waits around each year to catch the mercy in gray Spring
April skies
As the thunder roars and lightning cries his life's rages, he embraces
that scared weeping little boy inside and dries his eyes through the
escape of his own adult tears
As GOD's showering the earth, he takes the opportunity to relinquish
and bury his hurts and fears into the concrete and dirt
Forced to find solace in the storm because the sunshine usually hurts
for a man forced to compromise his heart just to maintain his worth
But when he performs in the ways of which he's been programmed he
realizes he's been set up to be labeled another emotionally unstable
black man
With no one to turn to because the world has turned its back and
there's no one to hold his hand

Not even his mom and dad
But if a sociopath isn't what you wanted for a son, then a sociopath isn't what you should have raised him as
And because of your mistakes, for him its too late
Now he's treated as if he's a home-made manufactured enemy of the state
He's now a menace to society
Fucked by this society
Screaming fuck a society that will rob you of your birthright with pre-ordained stigmas, stereotypes and ideologies
When all he wanted was to be free and able to express himself
But when his heart was forced to be hidden in a cage
His rage put another Nigger behind bars
So today another black man became a slave

Bodies Sleeping with a Dead Body

No faces or personalities
Just anatomies, of whom sometimes I don't even know their names
Only identifying skin's textures, body curvatures, scent of pheromones and planes
Heated bodies and ideas manifest beyond our brains as the fire raises a different temperature in each flame
As our frames connect briefly our pictures temporarily become one in the same
Exchanging bodies and body fluids as sweat beads form storms like rain
Showering down on the body
And no matter how often someone lets their lusts shower down on my body
I only want for someone to not love me for physicality but as if I am somebody
I want to be loved
By somebody
I want to be hugged by somebody
Not just a fuck for somebody
I want to be more than just a body
I want to be more than just a hobby
Each time I lay with these beings that don't value my depth, I defile my own body
I default my own body
See, everybody shouldn't be allowed the access to lie down beside my body
Especially not those, who have no interest in knowing, what greatness may exist deep inside of me
But the fact is, there is nothing left inside me

There's only emptiness within my body
Because of me, my soul has become a victim of robbery
So I am nothing more than an unburied corpse for the living to have access to my body
I guess if I weren't so quick to accept everyone into my bed, my heart wouldn't have been up for constant rejection and denying
I've learned that when you're searching for love, you can't just operate with your body
So to all of those who've sought out sexual gratification through what appeared to be my human body
Who treated me as if I were no body
Who seen me as nothing... but just a body
Who didn't search for signs of life deep inside of me
I think it's time you realize your perversions of necrophilia... because you've been sleeping with a dead body...

Demons

I'm jogging in place
Face to face with these demons that I'm not prepared to confront yet,
so I sprint
Into lies and alibis as I dodge the truth
Fueling my mind and muscles with deceptive juice that will get me closer to the nearest escape route as I unknowingly start to drown on my own dishonesty
Flailing my arms about for help but there's no lifeguard on duty, there's just me
There's just me and my demons
About my ankles I feel them creeping and coming closer as I draw back and stare
They look just like me,
Offspring of myself,
I've produced them
(I've bought them here)
Unaware that my untreated wounds would leave an open canal for them to follow and contact me
But I'm not ready for this
I'm not prepared to face reality, so I run quickly to my falsehoods and fairy tales,
Anecdote and tall tales but still these demons are trailing me and haunting my existence
They refuse to quit, they're really quite persistent
I can't cope... and I refuse to co-exist so my minds drifts into 500 meter dashes of a dream
I begin chasing a peace that I can only envision so I take occupancy in residential fantasies

There I see that everything is beautiful for the moments that I choose to live in hiding
Afraid to sacrifice the fears of my truths so I continue fantasizing
Until a blinding darkness casts over me and I realize that my dream was just a nightmare disguising itself in pleasantries so that my demons can blindside me
They surprised me with the intentions to capture and kill me but I was able to shake myself free
Opened my eyes and ran that 500 meter dash, fast track back to reality
But I hadn't escaped, although I had shook them physically, they attached themselves to the soul of me and met me back in the conscious land of the living
Salivating and ready to swallow me whole and drink my blood as a libation
But I wasn't ready to die so I faced my demons head on and engaged this confrontation
And amidst our quarrel, I realized that I was fighting... with myself
I was running... from myself
I would have much rather killed my own self
Because I wasn't capable of loving myself
Despite my demons

Vacate

THE PERSON YOU'VE REACHED IS SOMEONE FROM WHOM
YOU'VE BEEN DISCONNECTED.
IF YOU FEEL THAT YOU'VE REACHED THIS MESSAGE IN ERROR...
YOU HAVEN'T!!!
I'M JUST DOING SOME RECONSTRUCTION IN MY LIFE AND
WHAT I'M BUILDING CAN'T STAND ON INCONSISTENCIES...
THEREFORE YOU'VE BEEN SET FREE,
RELEASED,
FIRED, OR WHATEVER TERM YOU'D LIKE, AS LONG AS YOU
KNOW THAT YOUR OUT OF MY LIFE... Away from me
Done Finito Kaput
See, I've set a torch to what we were and the only remnants that's left
is soot
Just a stain in my past that has taught me how to arrange my future
And though sutures have left scars from abrasions, without them, I
wouldn't know how to make it without you
See, you've bruised our possibilities
And although we can never be, you've taught me that it's my duty to
show another exactly how to love me
Because if I don't set the example of high standards for myself, then
how is someone else to treat me accurately
So I thank you
For purposely loving me improperly and doing it with no apology
So please stop calling me
I'm not buying anything that you have to say, remove me from your
call listing of telemarketing
See our parting, is such bittersweet sorrow because although I love
you forever and a day I know that I can't rely on you tomorrow

*No, I can't give you one more chance because I have no trust left for
you to borrow
Wait a minute... Let me check.... Yes I do
I have just a little bit of faith in you
To do exactly what I expect of you
To take my heart stitch it up just to reopen the wound again when you
break it in two
But you can't say that I didn't believe in you
And although I have forgiven, I'm sorry but there are no second
chances
Maybe your chances would have had a chance... If I hadn't already
learned my lesson
You've taught me well and my heart's been paying attention
So blame yourself for being such a good instructor...*

Freedoms Where I Want To Be... The Battle of Three

See, sometimes my mind is back in time, I'm still waiting for my emancipation
Slave to the brain
Whips and chains
I'm still waiting for Abe to sign the proclamation
No Harriet Tubman
No North Star
I'm still a slave on this plantation
But
Unlike the olden days
There's no whips and chains physically, simply I am my intimidation
I'm looking out at the others living life in elation
Watching from my mental cell block all my life where I've been stationed
Wishing it was just a bad dream or a bad scene on my TV screen and I can get up and turn the station
In my mind I feel like I'm serving time, I'm carrying the weight of an entire nation
Placing myself in this place where I don't want to be
Donnell Jones
He sung it wrong
If it were my song' it'd be called "Freedoms where I want to be"
Out of this box
No more slave to my caged mentality
They say this is the land of the free but my mind says that's fallacy
This challenge for me has been one of the hardest to overcome
But like that Old Negro Spiritual says, "We shall overcome", and then it finally says "some day"
And maybe my day hasn't come yet

Sometimes I wonder is this sing on "GOD can you hear me?" Mic
Check
Mic check 1
Mic check 1,2,1,2
And on to 23
Been praying the same prayer, all of my life and like Amistad, I just want him to "give us, us free"
And I say us because I know that this battle's not just being fought by me
It's like, I'm a slave stuck on my own plantation but who do I rebel against, when the slave master is me
The Battle of Three
(I) want to be set free but (Myself) won't let (Me)
GO

Adult Too Soon

*Don't put your pimp juice in my pudding pops
Or replace my leap pad for porn on a laptop.
I'm just a kid... I'm not interested in how to cook crack rocks
I like the sound of pop rocks
Not the alarming sounds of shoot outs and gun shots as bodies drop
and the sirens and services come to take us away
I just want to be a child, I want to laugh and play
I want to live in my innocence and illusion before reality takes my
virtues away
Could I please stay here in my room with my imagination just a little
bit longer before you decide to put me on a street corner?
Even in the summertime, I heard that it gets cold outside so I'd rather
stay here where it's warmer
Could I figure out my own dreams before you dress me up in garters,
g-strings and Maybelline and put me on stage as your performer
We're your sons and daughters, you're supposed to want a little bit
more for us
We want Blue's Clues and Dora The Explorer
Instead of federal investigations, crime labs, and reporters
If we don't have you then who's gonna support us
Don't force us to grow up too soon because adulthood is not for us
Remember those Crayola crayons that you bought us?
We'd rather use those to color outside of the lines instead of writing
notes of ransom or suicide
Don't choke a dream before they're even realized because soon after
subsides our ambitions as we travel on backward roads, with no
almanac, no map, and a misunderstood mission
Don't set me up to be another statistic*

Could you just "tell me how to get, how to get to Sesame Street" I just want to visit and learn to count to ten before the doctor tells me to "push" again

Just give me 10 minutes more to dream of being a track star before the judge starts running down my charges and multiple life sentences

You've got to give me positive influences and images of what you want my life to be

Because feeding negativity only breeds my tragedy

And the only person left to blame will be you... simply for creating... an adult to soon...

Judgment Pending

Improper actions
They treat me less than others because of my skin color
They treat me as if I'm an improper fraction
They discredit my race
The just might as well spit in my face
They tell me "to hurry up and buy and get out of my place"
My skin color, on their taste buds, has left a bitter and disconcerting taste
A hate of which they only know the secret recipe
And they've stirred the pot evenly
They've served their soup deviously
They want me to act vehemently so they speak to me ignorantly
As if I don't have the ability
To control myself physically
As if I lack complexity
To talk to them brilliantly
But I guess my skin tone discounts that fact that I have a college degree because they still deny me
No manners and morals can rectify me
I'm a color stained canvas in their eyes and nothing can purify me
But as much as they try to crucify me
I know that GOD created me through his infinite power and divinity
And it's in him where I find my validity
So if they didn't have the power to breathe life into me then they don't have the power to condemn me
Your motions been denied
My judgment's still pending

Dear Whoever

Dear Whoever
I think that it's best that I write a letter
Because sometimes I can't vocalize and I don't know how to make it better
So I'm going to put pen
To paper
And waver the use of my diaphragm and try to cram all of my thoughts upon these pages
Because my heart's breaking and I don't know how to save it
My souls moving closer to the edge of the ledge and I want to let him go so I'm writing him this letter because I don't know how to say it
For so long, I've slept comfortably in the arms of murder without turning him in
Prepare my sentence as I prepare my sentence and give my confession
I've lessened myself because I didn't love myself
My soul died at the stake of my own insecurities
I've walked on hard, broken brick and I see that their characteristics mimic and mirror my identity
So Dear Lover
It had nothing to do with you, I just couldn't give my heart to you because it was already damaged and bruised
So when I met you it was long buried 6 feet under in the cemetery of tragedy
See, I grew up in a household where love was the equivalent of assault and battery
So if you want to blame someone, you should start with my daddy
Who started with my mother, and then with my brother
And I was his offspring so I was guilty automatically

And sometimes I just think things would've been better if life didn't have me
And we could all imagine me
The possibilities of what could be
But this is life and this is me
I can't just pack up my soul and leave my problems behind as I move into another body
Speaking of bodies
It became a hobby for me trying to find myself deep within the loins and in the grips of another person's skin
Unlike you, my dear friend, love never loved me in the places that I thought it was owed to me so I went out and tried to find it in sex drugs and sin
E pills and alcohol and orgies with her, her and him
A bunch of lost lonely souls searching for acceptance in a world so gruesome and grim
In dim lit rooms contemplating lethal injections to bring about the onset of my emancipation
So Dear Nation
Don't continue waiting for me because I don't know if I'll make it
I have so much to give but misery has awakened in me and I don't know if I can take it
Aching from the ridicule of my peers so over the years I became numb
The use of drugs become my medication, separation and my fun,
But the fun ended when I blacked out and found myself standing over a man whose face reminded me of a high school bully, as I aimed at his head with my gun
So Dear Son, of the man I murdered, I'm sorry that you will be forced to grow up like me
Trying to find your way, as a man without the guidance or positive influence of a daddy

Feeling like your missing the love of the ones that you loved automatically
Trying to mend the pieces to a shattered and broken family to no avail
Feeling as if you've failed
Finding yourself in your own personal jail because misery's prevailed, I've taken that route and when you give into desolation, the only option is a tragic end
Write you're past a goodbye letter and pen the path to chapters of your future where peace begins
And title it Dear Serenity... This is where misery ends

Fuck Boi

Fuck Boi
Fashioned in fallacy
Telepathy of the true definition of nigger breaches the makings of a real man's true mentality
So he lives up to the expectations of everything that the white man said that he could be
"A fuckin' Nigger"
But in retreat of the derogatory I'll just call him Fuck Boi
Not much sweeter than his slave name but Nigga is a word that I choose not to employ
Dopeboy dishing death, to subsequently remain detained in dungeons
In pursuit of something that he valued because he believes that the almighty dollar would set him free
Unaware that the price of simple green paper could be so costly
Because the eyes of a Fuck Boi can only see jewelry, flashy clothing, and quick pussy
Thusly, these women become his bitches
And these bitches become his toys
Playing with her heart because emotionally he's void
She's the action figure, enjoyed by this "I don't give a Fuck Boi"
Destroyed by his careless antics but she keeps him around because she says "he's got some good Fuck boi"
Dick of a dope boy, getting high on his own supply
Eventually his sources run dry and he becomes a stick up boy robbing his own people to get by
Experimenting with genocide and expecting his hood to respect him
Question
Why the Fuck Boi?
You've destroyed your own kind, just so that you can still come up, boy

Got 5 little boys, who need your love and you still don't give a Fuck Boi
Dismissed wisdom because you're content being ignorant, when clearly you can never know enough boy
Slave to a mental Fuck Boi
Bed wench to the white man's ideas, I hear Massa callin' on your knees, face down ass up, boy
Fine with being a representation of a good nigga so you continue to take the whippings of a slave
No physical slave master but the contentment of being a nigga and the actions of select individual is enough to keep a people caged
Fuck Boi decaying all that our ancestors fought against you commence to rebuild
Fulfilling an unwritten will, with lack of knowledge, lost heritage, and selfishness is enough to get us killed... by each other
Soon enough we will be extinct and our blood will be on the hands of another murdered brother
Discover murder weapons in the shallow hearts of yourselves
Still intangible because your depth only deepens with the trappings of the singular physical wealth
No love but relentlessness is "the shining" I see sparkling in your eyes... REDRUM REDRUM
No fucks are given to the loss of our generation, as long as this Fuck Boi gains everything he wants
So it's simple, you don't hunger for much, boy
This world is swallowing you whole, had your body for breakfast and it's gonna digest your soul for lunch, boy
But you dont give a Fuck Boi
You just want to Fuck Boi
Already fucked yourself as you fuck, and you Fuck Boi
Diseases in your nut boy
But raw you still Fuck Boi

Continue living for yourself today and all of our futures will be fucked, boy

Little Box

Trouble brews for one who's insecure which gives birth to mythology,
which develops images and ideas so falsified its folklore
Guaranteed is not a happy ending
Only available is a negative plot
See What I've got is a heart so fragile, and it's been bruised and beat by stone
Damn near dedicated to tragedy
The thought of trust I've disowned
And I've made me a home here in this little box
Shit... found me a throne here in this little box
Breeding a complex in my home within the walls of this little box
See toxic is my mind, its venom so strong
A genuine tune can be vocalized right in front of me and yet I'd examine its song
And I know that I make it hard for someone to truly love me
But I've got to protect the biggest asset and value of me

Broken Poetry

Attracted to your fearlessness
Attracted to your heart
Attracted to you physically
Connected through our art
Through tattoos and poetry, we formed a common bond
Imprinted in my mind because our ways drifted apart
And even though we parted ways, you will always be a part of me
And every time I step on stage, I'll think of you when I spit this poetry
See
I said "spit" this poetry
You were the first to inspire me to open up my mouth so that the world could feel what lives within the soul of me
But right now, I say this woefully
Because I always hoped that we'd cross paths again but now that's just a dream that will never be
Logged on to facebook today and the caption below your image, read
R.I.P
Rest In Peace
I thought there's got to be some type of malfunction because this can't be
Not my friend
Not K.P
We lost touch for two years and now my only option is for you to live within my memory?
And although thoughts are alive and well, I don't know if they'll suffice because they'll always live intangibly
It just saddens me that I'll never reach you in this life again
So, I'm woefully submitting poetry and instead of ink you will only find manuscripts of tears on pages from the ball point of my pen

Agony seeping painfully through me like tattoo needles and piercings through skin
Ripping directly through the depths of me to the place where my love for you, and my love for these lyrics began
So, as I step up on stage, I'm giving them my all in a manner in which a poet is supposedly
The only difference today is, no water will emit
Only blood will I spit
From my heart as I transmit this Broken Poetry

Teardrops in a Shot Glass

Filling empty spaces with useless matter because she longs for something more

But those empty places are just as hollow and vacant as they were before

She can't endure, so she finds another lonely body in hopes that it can fill her at the core

That one couldn't do it, so she invited more and more to her skin

Connections through sexual affections, she thinks that there's no way that she can't win

And yet again her body's pleased but his penis missed the mark within

It couldn't touch her heart or gravitate to her soul

Becoming fed up with life and she wants to let go, but her conscience says no

And she cries yet another tear in a shot glass

Heart so broken that it can't be healed by triple by-pass

And each time her heart takes shot after shot, up again goes her shot glass

College graduate but ways to mend a broken heart wasn't taught in her psych class

So she becomes drunk off of these liquors of life as time passes by and she hopes that these alcohols can heal her

Medicating herself through bodies and manmade remedies, raise your hand if you can feel her

Paint the picture clearer and you can see all of her hues

Illustrated in colors of blacks and blues

Heart so broken from being stomped and misused

And the bruising is visible, but she uses alcohol to heal it

Believing that if she drinks enough, that she will no longer feel it

But she's only bringing herself to an early grave by being paralyzed by her fears

*She's drowning in the waters of life and the proof is self evident and made tangible by her own tears
And her ways of coping only offers her a false sense of comfort and more problems to face
Then again goes another shot glass to her face
But there's nothing left, only the salt of her tears can she taste*

Who's Gonna Love Me?

I wonder... Who's gonna LOVE me
Because... if this is love... then hate me please
Prayed so much for us that concrete has left its bruised signature upon my knees
I guess that's my receipt to trade your hate back in for my heart
Oh I almost forgot that this is what you call love, that's why Cupid never appeared with bow and arrow, but instead with bandages and darts
Leading me on and slowly killing me as you kissed me with decaffeinated kisses
Gave me artificial flavors but the natural sweetener and sugars were missing
Left me hung over and intoxicated from what you were giving
Not the sweetness of candy but instead the sickness of poisoning
As I drank myself silly with hope, searching to find the proper high on your love
But the love you showed took me so low that there was only a bed of grass and a tombstone above
And the inscription read
"Love Dead"
Loved another so much that I forgot to love me
Became so desensitized and googly eyed that I didn't realize that you were administering something that love would never serve me...
which earned me the right to recite
(singing) "Don't you remember?"
"Don't you remember the reason you loved me... before?"
"Baby please remember... me... once more"
It's simple, you can't remember something that was never there, but I thought that you loved me

I THOUGHT THAT YOU LOVED ME
But you only gave me fairy tale I love you'S and there was no happy ending because you never truly cared to share your heart with me
This is why I sit here in this clinic, wondering why the one to whom I was committed could have possibly given me H.I.V
But you said that you loved me
YOU SAID THAT YOU LOVED ME
But this only proves that hate can hide its hues when love is only used to produce beautiful wording
Now I guess that I can only rely on me to truly love me
...If not...
THEN WHOS GONNA LOVE ME...

The Way We Paint

We've vandalized our world with hate
Lost all regard for humanity and put it into this place where there's no grace there
Wailing fills the air
Sirens fill our ears, as tears fall from faces
We think that we've settled scores but war and turmoil is what evil wages
And we gain nothing but pain and suffering, heartache and lost wages
Bodies in bags, bodies in cages
See, I'm still trying to figure out where peace and persecution became correlated
The beauty of the world is fading, and yet we continue to dance to the jailhouse rock
When everyday another body is being locked away in a casket or being placed upon a cell block
But when does it stop?
When do we stop killing and enslaving ourselves
When will we stop being generous enough to give death to another but not selfish enough to give an opportunity to ourselves
See, our lives are like a book, but we've bound ourselves between its pages when making bad decisions, it's like closing together the covers and our futures become suffocated
How heartbreaking it is to look into the faces of our beautiful children and realize that our future is fading...
If only I had the power to save it
If I could... I'd paint it
I'd paint a cold world a warm heart
Fill it with love and erase hate's graffiti marks
And I'd trace it with respect, tolerance and appreciation

Reflect exactly what GOD IS...
LOVE would radiate all throughout the illustration
Unity would run free, no more division within our nation
We have the power to ink a wonderful world
We've just got to start painting...
Beautifully

Just to be loved

Just to be loved, I've disposed of myself like yesterdays garbage
Dishonored my own reflection, afraid that no one else would want it
Painted myself in the letter 'A' of Scarlet simply because I've fucked myself for someone else, Just to be loved with no commitment
Just to be loved, I've been committed to insane asylums that housed promises of forever in the confines of mental prisons
Just to be loved like the religions of Muslims, Jews and Christians
I've been seduced by cold hearts and concrete kisses
Burglarized by false teeth of false smiles with true motives hidden behind contact lenses that said I just want to steal your heart...
So, I gave it up under false pretences, in hopes that I'd get something back in return
Just to be loved, I placed the core of myself in urns as the remains burned and my essence turned into ashes
Holding on to hope in my sight and hiding my hurt behind eye patches
Just to be loved, I've tucked away the baggage in internalized compartments so that no one can see the damage
And I've managed to feel no less than a penny with a hole in its center with no bandage
Just to be loved, I've learned to mute my emotions and express myself through these closed captions
Just to be loved, I've invited multiple bodies to my mattress just to eliminate our lonesome
Longing to be wanted, the little boy in me invited strangers to the home front just so that someone would be there to hold him
Morals, I tucked and folded away, just to be loved I was willing to disown them
Placed heavyweights on my shoulders as my hands and arms swam for hearts in tandem

Set myself up for ransom just to be loved with reckless abandon
Couldn't ever imagine that if ever I were looking for love the almighty wouldn't be the answer
Because "Jesus loves me this I know, for the Bible tells me so"
And I'd hate to feel that, that isn't so, but why do I feel damned by some of its stanzas
I tired of searching for something just to always feel abandoned
Just to be loved, I lost my most broken part among the orphanage of hearts and when I learned to love myself, I went back and I found it
Just to be loved in the way that I deserve, which is unconditionally, because that's the only love that is true
So that's the only love that is valid

Adolescent Cosmetics

Flaws
Camouflaged in MAC make-up
Body draped in haute couture and expensive jewels to deflect her true make-up
Hiding in wigs and contact lenses, she likes to play dress up with multiple personalities
Today she's Vivian
Tomorrow she may be Valerie
A desensitized human being, representing multiple individuals existing in one body and each one is hiding from themselves
Rarely does she wear high heel shoes because they make it harder to run away from herself
A lesson she learned very well as a kid forced by daddy to dress up in mommies' undergarments and high heels
She stood paralyzed still in fear as poppa peeled away at her panties
Bending her at the waist, gripping her kinky bush and invading her anally
Painfully, she blamed herself, at fault was her femininity
So she deserted her true identity and acquired another until another became many
And eventually by the age of 17, she found the courage to run away with just her make-up, little money for a motel room and a new gown
Her father passed down to her the heart of a hustler so she found her place on the strip
Each night, she enticed men with a lollipop pursed between her lips
It was her scheme to get rich on every Tom that stuck his Dick in her Harry hole
Her money was her motivation to stay away from herself, and the consistent cash flow made it easier to accept a random man's load

Until she kicks him out and is left alone with just a semen stained mattress, a mirror and her make-up
Accompanied by the mental threats that were made by daddy's echoing voice and the sounds of the multiple personality's that she's made up
Welding up with tears as the Valeries and Vivians die as she washes her face to remove her mask
Looking in the mirror while slowly unfolding is her past as she pulls the silicone pads from the bra upon her chest
She pulls the halter from around her neck and steps out of her dress and stares at the little boy that's she lost and loathed for longer than four years
Standing there in the same position of which she left him, scared and shaken by his fears
Looking in the mirror, she wrapped her arms around herself and decided that it was time that he lived
Despite what happened to him in the past he was ready to love himself again when he removed the mask of make-up of a scared adolescent Hidden in cosmetics...

Predestined Hell

Positioned myself on the edge of glory
Told stories in allegory, to avoid the judgment of an unjust jury
Purely to protect my image from equivalent sinners whose fire has no fury
Though injurious mentions caused me to bleed like painful incisions of a main artery
Kleenex to stop the blood and tears but tissue wasn't able to prevent the scarring
And amidst the painful words I lost me
Somewhere in between the actions of nouns and verbs
Still I planted good seeds upon barren earth but somehow inbred a curse, when ...I was preserved for greatness
Find Beliefs that aren't identical to religious idealists then you're somehow considered atheist, when my faith has been centered around truth and spirituality
Those same Sunday morning church goers, who claim to pray for me, have been the same judgmental sinners who callus me
Unable to recognize their own faults because they're too busy pointing out another's immoralities and challenging their belief
Despite my faults my faith remains in my heart, locked in for safe keeps
And although I believe in all that the biblical book speaks, that doesn't mean that I agree
An issue between myself and the almighty that causes my soul to weep as I bleed and excrete pain upon poetic pages and psalms
The type of sinner that I am will not inherit the heavenly Kingdom so why not allow me happiness here in my earthly home
Where my soul roams and remains wounded by words of the creator whom I feel has turned His back on me

They say that the gift of life is a blessing but I feel that my birth was a pre-destined tragedy
So I breathe, inebriated breaths to escape this reality, where human beings and their higher powers feel that I am not good enough
A fucked up existence
Was already fucked and damned before my fucking existence
This wasn't my fucking decision
But somehow I have to pay the fucking price
The wages of sin is death so I guess its fuck my life
And I'm expected to see that the sunlight succeeds the rain but how can I when my life has been forecasted among clouds
Lord, I hear the sounds of blessing
But I see the scriptures and what I feel approaching is death
It would have probably been best if I were birthed in a body bag, because my casket was already pre-set
There's nothing left
Except my predestined hell

Untitled

The trigger fingered his failure
Evidence of murder pierced like thrusts of painful impalers
His existence is Gilligan's Island and he's lost like sailors
Momma's a good Godly woman; she listened to the music of Mahalia Jackson
Hailing all the way from Jackson Mississippi,
she poured love in his Sippy Cup but now it's blood that he's dripping from his lips
A sick depraved craving
Despite his bad decisions, a mother's love for her only baby has her gravely aging
She's been praying and it's the only way she knows to save her son
Her body is becoming numb because her heart's on the run and her love is not strong enough to save him
She blames herself, tracing back trying to find the misstep, where she went wrong when raising him
Gazing at what the world sees as the monster on the TV screen, she only recognizes her little boy
Still her pride and joy and although he disappoints her, she's never ashamed
In fact, she believes that she's the blame from separating him from his papa
But to keep him around would ensure the death of his mama and the uncertainties of who was going to raise her son
She wasn't prepared to allow that to happen, so one morning before he went off to work she took her final beating
It had something to do with mama overheating his toast
He pistol whipped her, as their son stood close and cried as daddy administered another beating

She decided then that she was tired of a man who was supposed to love her constantly mistreating
Once he departed, she kneeled at her son's side with swollen and bleeding eyes and explained to her scared little boy that his daddy would be leaving
She needed him to understand but her 7 year old couldn't determine why, the man that he respected loved and idolized had to go
And mamma saw it to be imperative for her safety and her child's future to extricate this bad example
Once papa returned home the fight continued about something that began that morning
He attempted to raise his hand at her but she pulled a gun from beneath her housecoat, cocked it back and she gave him full warning
Her little boy THEN realized exactly what mama meant when she said that daddy had to go
He ran from his room into the hallway where the fight was taking place, gripping his father's legs, begging them both "please don't"
His eyes were fixed upon her
Her eyes were affixed upon him
And their little boy's eyes saw life escape daddy once mamma pulled the trigger, close range, and left two bullets in his chest
Daddy fell back and mother and son stood there dazed and in silence
Eventually the sound of sirens forced them to hustle and dispose of the body
She forced her son to grab his father's feet as they rushed his corpse behind their home and dumped it into a creek
She escaped the possibilities of being prosecuted but in turn she took the charge of an angry and troubled son
Now the little boy who she tried to protect is a serial killer on the run, taking his vengeance out on the world because he's unable to face his problems
And since neither of them could, it's up to the authorities to solve him

As his face flashes across the screen, she still refers to the man that
America sees as a killer and coward, as her baby
Although it couldn't save him, that love that she reserved in her heart
for him is indefinite and unchanging
Her love for her son is always remaining...
Even if it kills her

Written In Blood

Ashes to ashes
Dust to dust
Paper to Passion
Pen inks blood
Sincerely with love
If ever you're looking and can't find me
My heart can be found disintegrated upon pages of poetry
The only DNA that knows me and holds me close, comes from stains of my own broken skin
Penetrating forearms and wrists deep enough, just so that I can feel that warmth, that burn that I've been longing for within
Dissecting through epidermis layers so that someone else can see that I have a heart too
And it's filled with ink that feeds the veins that leaks as I write "Dear John Doe letters to myself
like
"Dear bruised being
The hurt will shortly be leaving as the oxygen defies your body
The crimson tide will no longer send waves crashing through your anatomy because your heart will deny the study of hematology
This diabolical existence shall cease in the fate of this biology
And soon... you will die
Probably before you sign your final goodbyes, you will expire in the way that you've always wanted to exist... with your heart cradled in someone's hands
The only hands that were able to understand you and express your emptiness will now be responsible for you emancipation

Those hands that have abruptly eliminated your pain are now at fault for the lost life that drips from the pen nestled between your fingertips"
In a panic, I drop my pen and look down at my wrist and see that I've inked my own end
But this is not a suicide note because I don't want to die
I'd rather a mother come to my rescue and hold me close like back before umbilical cords are cut and babies are forced to learn to walk upright
I want a love to come along with a power so strong that it could heal these abrasions in my skin of which my life cries
I want a happy ending and lullabies that won't lull me back to sleep but bring me back to life
My body's feeling tired and my head is feeling light as this blood runs from my arms, forming a bath beneath me
As life is excreting, I flashback to a deceased father that will probably meet me for my greeting
Because the life is leaving me and there's no brothers or sisters that can save me
DNA made us relative but even blood consistency is subject to changing
And in those brief moments of evaluating and waiting for someone to find me, I realized that I needed to find myself
Stopped worrying about who didn't and who wouldn't love me and realized that I needed to love myself
Picked up my pen and walked to the door to explore a new life and an internal wealth
But by the time I turned the knob, I had already fallen victim to my fears...
My soul flew away and left my tattered and lost corpse waiting here to be discovered by someone who'd wrap me in a basket hold of love

But only death came to find me, with my pen and my letter... written in Blood....

Contact Information

Contact Kevin Wiggins on:

Facebook

www.facebook.com/kevin.themysfitwiggins

email

mysfit87@yahoo.com

www.ingramcontent.com/pod-product-compliance
Lightning Source LLC
LaVergne TN
LVHW011355080426
835511LV00005B/294